Published by: Eva Bodfäldt Education
www.evabodfaldt.com
ISBN: 978 91 973578 5 2

Translation: Mona Lindau-Webb, Charlotte West and Robbin Battison
Photography: Åsa Lindholm
Graphic design: Märta Segerström
Printing: Livonia Print, Latvia

Follow Me

– a Deal with Your Dog

Eva Bodfäldt

EVA BODFÄLDT

INTRODUCTION

All roads lead to Rome. There is not just one truth, nor just one method for success in raising and training your dog. Personally, I strive to be proactive rather than reactive. A proactive trainer is a facilitator who focuses on education by rewarding and reinforcing desired behaviors, while a reactive trainer corrects and scolds. My goal in this book is to not only describe practical steps on how to train your dog, but also to communicate how your own outlook can affect your dog and your relationship.

I would like to acknowledge Anders Hallgren, the maestro who encouraged me to write this book. Thanks to Bob Bailey and Marian Bailey for their willingness to share their knowledge about learning theory. I would also like to express my gratitude to my editor Eliza Kajanus, photographer Asa Lindholm, and to designer Märta Segerström. I would like to thank Mona Lindau-Webb, who put her training knowledge to work when she translated the Swedish book into English, and to Joanna LeBlanc, Charlotte West and Robbin Battison for their joy, knowledge and stubbornness in the final editing of Follow Me. Thanks to my wonderful mother for teaching me that nothing is impossible. And most of all thanks to all of you whom I have met and taught – without you, *Follow Me – a Deal with Your Dog* would never have been written.

Contents

Who Follows Whom? About Training for Contact and Willingness to Follow

Contents:

The goal for most dog owners is an obedient dog who follows, pays attention and maintains contact. The dog must be sensitive and attentive and ask for permission before he pulls away. Most people agree this is the ideal pet. But how do we achieve this outcome? There are many different ways to instill obedience. Your chosen method often depends on your value system. There are people who consider dominance to be the foundation the human's relationship to the dog; the dog must submit. My belief is that you will get much further by building on the dog's spontaneous desire to maintain a connection. Contact with your dog opens up communication and therefore paves the way for further learning.

WILLINGNESS TO FOLLOW – YOUR DOG'S DESIRE FOR SPONTANEOUS CONTACT

A dog who is willing to follow spontaneously makes and maintains contact with you without being told. He pays attention to what you do, not vice versa. This dog follows you without being called or using the leash. He immediately notices any change of pace or direction while being walked; other dogs will just continue.

Training your dog to follow and be obedient is an enormously important foundation for all owners, whether your pet is a companion, a show dog, a hunting dog, or working dog. A dog with these qualities is sensitive to what you want and is better at focusing and learning new tasks. This training is the foundation for all further training as it is based on communication and teamwork.

Are you with me? May I…?

Dogs all have their own ways of seeking contact with you. Some will just glance over their shoulder to check that we are there. In that glance is a question – what are we doing? Are you with me? May I…? Some dogs may keep in touch by stopping, waiting for us for a short greeting, and then continuing onwards while wagging their tail. Others will come up to our side and beg for attention. Other dogs do not really look at us, but they will hear where we are and stay close without running off out of sight.

Ginza, my friend's Terveuren (Belgian sheepdog), will jump on you and put her front paws on your stomach when you aren't paying attention. What a spontaneous greeting! We can see how her eyes sparkle when she hits the bull's eye, knocking the air out of you. Then we playfully bark back at her and she continues on her way, joyfully wagging her tail. I can almost hear her whistling happily to herself.

Willingness to follow is natural for the dog

The language of following and contact is much more natural to a dog than our human language, which largely consists of spoken words. Following each other is natural for dogs. They trail behind their mama when they are little, and then they follow their pack.

But dogs also follow us as we fulfill their need for security, play and activity. Unfortunately, as dogs get older, we often cease to acknowledge their natural, spontaneous obedience. Instead, we use words and signals, because we decide that the dog is old enough to understand English. By and by, we forget to use the kind of language that was natural for us when communicating with them as puppies. However, training for willingness to follow is not just for young dogs, but instills a lifelong form of communication. You should continue to be bilingual with your adult dog!

Good contact and maintaining a connection is not about commands

My first interest in the relationship between dog and owner is the number times contact is sought and who takes the initiative. The owner who inundates the dog with a lot of spoken commands and prohibitions seldom has a good relationship with his or her pet. On the contrary, calmness is often what characterizes a good relationship between a person and a dog. This type of dog owner does not say very much; instead the dog initiates most encounters. Constantly recalling the dog actually decreases the dog's desire for contact.

IN TOUCH WITH YOUR DOG – IT PAYS TO PAY ATTENTION

In order to foster willingness to follow, obedience and cooperation in my dogs, I teach them a simple rule. *Look here for positive reinforcement. It pays to pay attention!* I don't give the dog any signal – I reward its own spontaneous initiative to make contact. This creates teamwork and is a win-win situation. I learn to read my dog's signals and to understand them, and I get a pet who obeys with joy. The dog learns to be attentive and in return has more freedom. This is what I call "making a deal with your dog", and for me this is not a training exercise – it is the whole foundation for how I view the relationship between humans and their best friend.

FOLLOW ME!
Look here for positive reinforcement. It pays to pay attention!

Who follows whom?

Maintaining a connection with your dog means rewarding his spontaneous desire to make contact by offering something that is important to him, rather than just teaching him to obey a signal or command. You teach the dog that it pays off to look at you or approach you without a signal. You shouldn't coax the dog when he is occupied elsewhere – then who is initiating contact? Regardless of if you are on a walk or training for obedience competition, the basic principle is the same – the dog is the one who should actively seek you out to play, cuddle or get a treat.

Reward desired behaviors

When you start training your dog, the dog's only role is to make spontaneous contact without any signal from you. It may, for example, stop and look at you, or approach your left or right side. As soon as the dog makes contact, reward the behavior. Being willing to follow must pay off for the dog – only then will he increase how often he initiates contact!

Think about this:

How many times an hour does your dog make contact while inside the house?
How many times within a five-minute period do you make contact with your dog while inside?
How times does your dog spontaneously contact you when you are quiet?
Who breaks off contact first?

DOES IT PAY TO FOLLOW? THE REWARDS MAKE THE DIFFERENCE!

When training your dog to be willing to follow, it is important to offer him enjoyable and exciting rewards. Start with what your pet really likes! The dog – not you – is the one to decide if it is worthwhile to follow you. Vary the treats you use to keep the dog stimulated. Your own imagination should be the basis for making and maintaining contact.

A basketful of rewards

Imagine you have a basket full of rewards. When your dog initiates contact, choose something as a reward. You can for example…

- throw a treat for the dog to find
- hold the treat near your face, so the dog must work to get close
- throw a ball, either to the dog or behind you. This is an excellent reward when the dog initiates contact from distance by looking at you or moving towards you
- playfully bump your dog and at the same time joke with it in a happy voice
- sneak away like a panther when the dog looks at you, and then playfully throw yourself at him. You can also run the other way and let the dog chase you. Make rapid turns in a different direction when the dog approaches you. Don't stop until your dog has worked hard for a greeting, rest or more play.
- very quietly sit down when your dog looks at you. Do not coax the dog! Direct your interest at something on the ground or on something you have in your pocket, like a treat or a toy. Ignore your dog until he approaches.
- brush your dog, massage him, or scratch a favorite spot
- offer exercise. Doing a circus trick or an obedience exercise it enjoys is also a reward!

Think about this:

What is a reward for your dog? I usually give my class participants an exercise where they are to reward their dog in ten different ways without using treats – how many can you come up with?

CREATE A NEED TO BE CLOSE

Some dogs are more willing to follow than others. With hunting dogs, for example, one must count on spending a lot of time on training willingness to follow. Other breeds, such as herding dogs, have such a strong predisposition to keep the flock together that they can probably be said to be "born willing to follow". Such dogs would not require the same amount of training. But even within the same breed, individual predisposition can vary a lot between individuals.

Play hard to get

If you want to teach your dog to become willing to follow, you must foster his desire for closeness. If the dog does not spend meaningful time with you, his desire for closeness and spontaneous contact will decrease. Our faithful friend will start to look elsewhere for affection and entertainment.

For the dog, it is not the amount of praise, treats or play that is important to maintaining contact; the focal point is the effort he must exert to earn a reward. Be stingy with the goodies! The harder you make it for the dog to get to you, the more interest he will have, thus becoming more willing to follow. Play and cuddle with your dog – but make sure you interrupt the reward before your dog gets tired and turns away from you. For example, turn and walk away from the dog. If the dog departs in the middle of a reward, bump him in a playful way without any threat in your voice. If you allow the dog to interrupt your interaction, then you make it impossible to foster a need for more contact. In this case, your dog has already moved onto another activity that holds more interest than you.

Ruff does not want teamwork

Ruth came to me with a giant schnauzer named Ruff that had no interest in cooperating with his owner. He did not react positively to praise or petting; instead, his body would become stiff. Ruth was very active with her dog and trained Ruff so that she would be able to participate in obedience competitions.

We went for a walk. The dog was obviously independent and uninterested in his owner. It was Ruth who initiated contact, mostly in the form of praise and signals. We agreed to start from the beginning with Ruff. Ruth started treating him with indifference, both inside and outside the house, so that Ruff had to learn to fight for social contact. The effect was noticeable even after a couple of days. He started trying to get her attention. Only in those cases when Ruff imploringly wagged his tail and put his ears back did Ruth pay attention to him, and did not keep her interest up long enough for him to tire of it and leave her.

We also introduced new kinds of rewards for Ruff. No longer did he get treats for exercises he performed. Instead, he was rewarded when he displayed active begging behavior, for example by pulling back his ears and retracting the corners of his lips and wagging his tail with a low tail set. Ruff also had to learn that contact results in "please - go ahead". (Read more about the release signal "please – go ahead" in the chapter "Be a better teacher – about learning".)

Ruth started by making Ruff sit and placing a treat two feet in front of him in different situations. In the beginning, when he tried to steal the reward, she quickly snapped it up and waited quietly until Ruff understood that Ruth had the treat. After a couple of failed attempts, he understood Ruth was faster than he was and he gave up. He got his "please – go ahead" when he inquiringly sought her attention.

Ruth also started kneeling down and holding the treats in her teeth. He got his treat by actively making and maintaining contact with her by turning his head and getting close. Ruth continued petting him before he got his treat. If he then went away or became passive, Ruth would quietly turn away from him. He only got the treats when he responded to her petting and soft voice by not pulling away or becoming passive. At the same time, we reduced Ruff's food rations, so he would become even more motivated.

After four weeks of training, there was a drastic change in Ruff's behavior. When he wanted any form of attention or food, he displayed positive body language. He was much more attentive to Ruth and was considerably more responsive.

Why doesn't my dog think I am fun?

Sometimes I run into dog owners who behave in a way that would make any dog laugh his head off. But there are others whose dogs lackadaisically sniff the ground and do not seem particularly interested in what their humans are up to. We often become too intense when the dog's interest wanes. Our play and rewards lose their value if we use them to avert the dog's attention from something else.

Avoid demanding looks

As a young girl, I was taught not to look a dog straight in the eyes, as the dog might interpret that as a threat. Today I teach the meaning of eye contact that builds on trust and positive expectations rather than on demands. The dog that often experiences its owner's gaze as demanding will often demonstrate short, rapid eye contact. It is easy to misinterpret this as indifference. Therefore, do not make threatening glances at your dog, either during everyday activities or during training.

THE GENERAL: BASIC EXERCISE FOR WILLINGNESS TO FOLLOW

"The General" is a basic training exercise to foster willingness to follow. The goal is to teach your dog to actively seek eye contact when you stand still and quiet like a military general, so that you can reward, play or initiate a fun activity. This is an exercise based on maintaining contact: look at me for positive reinforcement.

1. Start at a short distance. The dog should be in front of you without any signal from you. Show the dog a treat or a toy and then hide it behind your back. Quietly wait for the dog to initiate contact. Immediately reward the dog when it does it right. Start in a calm environment, preferably indoors. Do not count on the dog looking you in the eyes the first time. Initially reward the dog when his gaze is above knee height. As soon as the dog understands, improve the exercise by only rewarding eye contact.

2. The next step is for your dog to keep his attention focused on you even when you don't have anything in your hands. Show the dog a treat or a toy. Turn away from the dog and simultaneously stuff the treat/toy in your pocket. Then stop your movement, stand up straight, and let your hands hang down along your side. Wait quietly for the dog to go around you and make contact from the front. Reward! This step is important, as many dog owners question why their dogs are so unfocused during training. A very common reason is that the dog thinks training is over when the owner no longer has anything in his or her hands.

3. At this point, change how you reward the dog by turning in the opposite direction when the dog looks at you. Hold the treat/toy close to your left leg. Move away with jerky movements, so the game becomes a chase where your dog has to fight to obtain the reward. This is more stimulating for the dog than simply giving the reward in front of you. When you give the reward from your left side, the dog will also learn that this is a positive position. This will be useful for you later on when teaching the dog to "heel".

4. Walk backwards with the dog with or without a leash, and do not give any signals. Give a reward when eye contact is made. Either give the dog something right away, or turn away so that the dog gets to chase his reward close to your leg.

5. The next step is to turn and walk away in the opposite direction. Does your dog come straight up to your side, making and maintaining contact? If so, offer a reward.

6. Now, add distractions. Does your dog still make contact with you in spite of environmental distractions, for example a person walking past? Reward!

Reading suggestions: You can read more about training with distractions in the chapter "Become a better teacher – about learning theory". In the booklet "Manual to In Touch With Your Dog – The Swedish Way" you can read more about contact and obedience exercises, and how to set goals in your training, as well as how to develop and expand these exercises.

SNEAK AWAY AND TEACH YOUR DOG TO FOLLOW

We frequently worry that our dogs don't come when called. Perhaps we should instead ask ourselves why the dog does not make contact with us more frequently. Why does he romp around on his own rather than staying close to us? Going for a walk often has a very different meaning for us humans than for our dogs. We want to exercise, meditate, and experience nature around us. To the dog, on the other hand, nature is an obvious place to chase odors and other sensations. However, it is next to impossible to forbid a dog to chase game without teaching it an alternative activity. Give the dog a task – checking up on you and preventing you from running away.

The Sneak-Away Method

A good way to teach a dog to be willing to follow and attentive is to vary direction and speed. If we always follow the same route or walk at the same speed, it becomes difficult for the dog to maintain contact – he always knows where we are. Instead, become unpredictable. When your dog walks calmly in front of you or becomes distracted by a smell, quietly and quickly sneak away. If you walk along a beaten track, you can suddenly step off into the rough. Continue in a different direction and find a good hiding place. Surprise! The dog does not know where you went.

Do not be afraid to use the dog's anxiety

Dare to make use of the anxiety that your dog experiences when he feels "lost"! This is not a particularly nice method, but it is very effective. Who wants to be left behind alone in the woods? The dog learns to stay close to you and make contact with you for fear you will suddenly disappear.

The fear of you suddenly going away will encourage behavioral change in your dog. He will start turning around and making contact to see if you are there. This is exactly the behavior to reward!

Create a need to be close.

Be quiet!

In order for the "Sneak Away" to work, you must do it in such a way that truly worries the dog. It is very important to stay quiet! Do not alert him before you sneak away. Your voice can easily tell the dog where you are.

Do not just hide when the dog runs away from you. If something else has caught his interest, your dog will hardly care that you sit hidden under a bush. You must sneak away even in calm situations in order to create some anxiety in your dog. If he does not maintain contact, make sure to disappear! This teaches the dog to keep track of where you are – not vice versa. The upshot will be a dog that often turns around to see where you are, and who will stay close – exactly what you want.

Do not let the dog find you every time

Vary the Sneak Away game so that sometimes your dog finds you and sometimes not. Always allowing the dog to find your hiding spot teaches it that it is a fantastic hunter and search dog. Now and then, when you notice that your dog is definitely worried, just step away and continue as if nothing had happened. This is the moment when a recall can be a wonderful feeling for the dog – saved! If you have a more independent dog, it is useful to comfort him, like "poor little guy who got left all alone in the big bad forest". This is a great way to reinforce the anxiety that the dog experienced when he had lost you.

The "Sneak Away" with a dog on leash

"Sneak Away" works even when your dog is on a leash. In my classes, I sometimes walk away from the rest of the group with a student and his or her dog. When the dog is not paying attention to his owner, I will grab the leash and slowly move forward. At the same time, I will continue to talk quietly to myself. The owner will stay quietly behind. In most cases, the dog will never realize the owner is lost as this has not happened before. After a couple of yards I stop. It often takes a while before the dog realizes his human is gone! He learns that he cannot lose sight of Mom or Dad or they will run away!

This is also a good exercise for the owners. The criterion for reward or recall is for the dog to make contact. If we call the dog at the "wrong" time, i.e. when he does not make eye contact with the owner, then it is up to me not to let him go.

Of course, the dog quickly learns that it is more fun to be with Mom or Dad, so this is a good time to increase the degree of difficulty by me offering the dog affection. The criterion is still the same: I will only let the dog go to his owner when he spontaneously interrupts his interaction with me and focuses on the owner. Then it is up to the owner to be a good playmate to keep the dog engaged. If the owner remains silent, I will continue playing with the dog. In this way, the dog learns which signal will result in permission to run back to his person.

This exercise functions as a continuation on the "usual" Sneak Away exercise as it deals with increasing amounts of distractions.

Vary the rewards...

Reward making and maintaining contact in all the different ways you know your dog loves. Avoid using the same tone of voice and type of reward every time. Be a clown! What happens if you are "caught"? Surely, you will not be happy if your prison guard finds you? Maybe pretend you are aghast the dog found you. What happens if you playfully bump your dog when he gets close to you and then run away?

Training tips: Activate the dog before training

Most dogs have more energy at the beginning. It can be hard to do exercises like "Sneak Away" to encourage contact and following ability before your dog has calmed down a bit. Therefore, begin the walk with an activation exercise that requires your dog to work hard both physically and mentally. This will give the dog time to get rid of excess energy at the same time as you do something fun together.

A good way is Find It games! Have the dog search for a fun toy or a treat that you have hidden in trees and bushes or underneath a rock. Start by throwing out a couple of treats. Then let the dog loose and let him run around to find the treats. When the game gets more advanced, I will put out about 30 treats in a 60x60 foot area. This means it will take the dog a good while to find all the treats. I wait quietly until the dog has finished. The dog's activity level will determine how many treats I will use. If I notice that his intensity decreases, then I will continue on the walk. Someone else can get the remaining treats. The advantage in playing Find It with treats is that it will gradually increase the dog's stamina.

TREASURE HUNT: STAY CLOSE FOR EXCITEMENT

Sometimes the contact with the dog is intensive. Fall arrives and you are going to plant new bulbs for spring flowers. You work hard, you finish the work, and then you go inside to relax. The next morning you discover that your dog has dug up every single bulb you planted. Dogs do not see planted bulbs the same way we two-legged creatures do. Instead, things that have been buried are there to be dug up again. However, the dog's interest is not always met with understanding on our part. Eagerly, we try to shove the dog away. This will only increase his desire to share the experience with us. Anything we defend to the extreme degree of shoving surely must be something very important!

Even when we go mushroom picking the dog's interest in us may be greater than we would want. We move around, leaning forward, in a slow and focused way, searching the ground with eagle eyes. And look, here we find them, the fervently desired chanterelles! Immediately, as we start picking these treasures, four happy paws suddenly land in the middle of all the yellow. For the dog, there is no more committed teacher than a mushroom picker!

Invent a treasure hunt

Imagine if we could train the dog to be willing to follow with the same commitment and intensity as when we hunt for mushrooms or work in the garden. Show your dog it pays off to follow you in the woods. Invite him on a treasure hunt! Stop feeding the dog inside the house, and instead take dog's food to the woods. Sneak away from your dog, kneel down and pretend that you found food under a pine tree. When the dog comes, there are several ways you could act. You can pretend to be hungry and quickly "eat" the food. Then get up and walk away. At the same time, your dog will search the ground for leftover crumbs. Next time you sneak away, you may not be quite as hungry. When your dog approaches, you have found a bit more food you will not devour as quickly. Instead, get up and leave a little for your friend.

It doesn't always have to be food. Hide one of your dog's favorite objects and pretend you are sniffing for it. Do not look at the dog but focus on the ground, on a tree, or maybe a rock. Your dog will clearly understand this behavior, and it will increase his interest in staying nearby. After a while your dog will start searching in front of you, when he sees you walking and scanning the ground with your eyes. It has learned you are a fantastic hunter. Just in case there are treasures in your immediate vicinity, it might be a better idea to follow you than go off on a solo adventure.

Stormy's ball

On one occasion, I fastened a ball to a string, and threw it up a tree. Stormy caught the scent of this object and frantically tried to save the ball. I stood by quietly and curious as to how he planned to proceed with the rescue mission. His jumping was unsuccessful. The ball was too high up in the tree. He tried jumping from several angles before he caught sight of a rock about three feet from the branch where the ball was stuck. Stormy jumped up on the rock, but his first attempt was a failure, as was the second one. His third attempt succeeded. Stormy used the rock for take-off, snatched the ball during the jump and got hold of it. Great happiness for Team Bodfäldt – everybody cheered!

Find your inner child

Dogs often get a kick out of being with children. One reason is that children invent activities that arouse the dog's interest. As adults, we often turn our attention to the dog, but how much fun are we? Consider how a child behaves in the woods and compare it with ourselves. Find your inner child and your dog will really love you!

Kipling: a dog worth following

Dogs that live in a pack often stay together during walks. One of the dogs discovers an interesting scent; soon the other dog will join in. Together they analyze the smell. It is impossible for us to understand the extent of this cooperation. Even after just a few days in his family, retriever puppy Trolle already understood who was the most skilled when it came down to having a good time outdoors. Kipling, my older dog, did not deign the puppy even a glance, but went about as usual investigating his field-mouse holes. Suddenly he caught a scent and started digging intensively. Trolle gazed with wonder at Kipling's doings, only to seconds later throw himself down the hole to investigate the treasure Kipling had found. That was a big mistake! Kipling let out a deep roar. Little Trolle got himself out of the hole, as fast as he had thrown himself in there. He then watched Kipling from a respectable distance, until Kipling finally gave up. Then Trolle trundled over to the abandoned field-mouse hole, while at the same time keeping track of Kipling with side glances. After investigating the hole and the odors, he turned to see what Kipling was up to now.

It does not have to be any more difficult than this from a dog's point of view. A younger dog follows the one who keeps things exciting.

Training tip: Do not spend your whole walk training.

Do not spend the whole walk training but keep it to maybe fifteen minutes at a time. Then put the dog on the leash again. If you do not feel like training, make sure that you have your dog on a flexi-leash or long line so you do not lose the opportunity for exciting events. You have to be on your toes in order to succeed with the training, so be sure to finish up after a short while. The more willing to follow your dog becomes from all your exercises, the more you can just go on an "ordinary" walk.

KEEPING YOUR DOG IN LINE

There are many occasions where you cannot just let your dog loose. Maybe you have an independent dog who runs circles around you. In this case, it makes sense to use a long line for obedience training. You do this in the same way as training the off-leash dog. The difference is that, using the long line, you can immediately affect your dog's speed and direction.

The line – a training tool

How long a line to use depends on the size of your dog. In general, 60-70 feet is enough. Change to the line and then unhook the leash. Let the line trail on the ground behind the dog. Some dog owners claim that the dog does not understand that he has a line trailing behind him. I do not share that opinion. The dog is in fact inhibited when the line trails behind him. That is the whole point – we want to get more control over our four-legged friend. Used correctly, the line is a tool in obedience training. Just watch it so you do not become lazy and step on the line every time your dog catches sight of something he wants to chase. The extension may make you feel as though the line works as a bandage covering a wound. It feels nice and safe, but it will not heal the wound!

Change directions fast

Start the obedience training by unhooking the leash and attaching the line. Then turn quickly and take off in the opposite direction. Take care that the line trails along the ground without you holding it. When the dog passes you, step briefly on the line to break his speed. At the same time, quietly and decisively change direction, almost exaggerating it. This will surprise your dog. What on earth is Mom doing? Many dogs react by paying increased attention to changes in your movements. Be sure to reward this spontaneous contact! Repeat this training until your dog no longer dashes past you but instead initiates contact. Now you have done about 10% of the job. The dog has stopped dashing past you. You have accomplished a temporary slowing of speed – important, but temporary. The next step is to teach your dog which behavior will reap greater rewards, i.e. keeping within a certain distance from you and keeping the same speed as you, regardless of whether you are standing still or moving. Teach your dog that it pays off to spontaneously stop and make contact with you, and to slow down, and to turn and get back to you without you telling him anything.

Not every dog can be let off-leash

Many factors decide if you will succeed with off-leash training. How much time do you have? Even your choice of breed is important. If your dog has been bred from pure hunting lines, or if your breed is well known for independence, then it will take more extensive training to teach the dog to hang around Mom and Dad. Be realistic! Not every dog can be let off-leash. Dogs who are usually on leash must be given opportunities to run. Running beside you on a bicycle is one way to do this. Some dogs may be off-leash for a short time provided they have a defined task. For example they can run between family members to play or get treats, they can play with another dog, or search for something.

Reading suggestion: More contact exercises for practicing with your dog on-leash can be found in the chapter "Obedient on-leash – about teaching the dog to heel".

TRAIN THE DOG TO BE WILLING TO FOLLOW ON THE TRAINING GROUND

Sometimes it is hard to teach obedience on training grounds with other dogs present. Your dog may not be trained for major environmental distractions and may therefore have problems absorbing the training. There are simply far too many things to look at. Mom is on the other end of the leash, so there is no need to pay attention to her.

Leo - focus results in rewards

I meet Maria and Leo, an 18-month-old male Rottweiler, during a course for Doggie Delinquents. While I am explaining an exercise to the students in the class, I see from the corner of my eye how Leo repeatedly tries to leave Maria. She responds by standing there, jerking now and then on Leo's collar. Leo gradually becomes more impatient and active and Maria becomes increasingly irritated. Curses are about to fly. I ask Maria calmly and silently to walk up to the fence a couple of yards away and tie Leo up. This changes the situation completely. As soon as Maria ties up Leo and leaves him, he plaintively searches for her. I ask Maria to let a rain of treats pour over Leo. Surprised and happy, he starts searching for the treats. He learns in a flash that there will be a rain of treats that he can search for – if he looks at Maria. Building on this contact training, Maria places a bowl of treats on the training grounds. She unties her dog from the fence and waits for Leo to look at her. As soon as he tries to make eye contact, Maria gives him permission and runs with him to the bowl of treats.

Tie up the dog

Sometimes your dog forgets that he belongs to your family, and in such cases, a good way to train him is to do as Maria did and tie him up, as in the previous example. Stand a couple of yards in front of him. Stay calm and do not stare. What kind of emotion do you want to transmit? Find an emotion yourself! What will happen is that the dog will gradually calm down and focus when you adopt this particular body posture.

Reward the dog, regardless of whether he stands, sits or lies down. The main idea here is that the dog looks at you attentively without barking or whining. You may throw some treats to your dog the first couple of times, particularly when you plan to approach him. That minimizes the risk of him barking.

As soon as you see your dog understands the task by looking at you and remaining silent, then it is time to take the training to the next level. As soon as the dog tries to make eye contact, offer him an activity that he enjoys. This can be play, a circus trick, or an obedience exercise he already knows.

If the dog loses his focus on you, depart in a friendly but firm way. In this way, your dog will learn to call you back by making eye contact and being quiet. Your reward will be a more focused dog, which you do not need to nag and correct for lack of attention.

Training tip: Train in short spurts

Train your dog only for a minute or two at a time, but train frequently and vary the pattern. A dog that is not used to mental stimulation does not have the power to focus for very long.

Time Out

Your dog is the one who is going to make contact with you, not vice versa. If you have to jump and bounce around in order for the dog to even notice you and make contact, you are actually rewarding inattentiveness. Therefore, you must first figure out what it is that makes the dog want to seek contact.

If the dog loses all interest during the training session, you can use a time out and leave him alone for a while. Tie him up or signal "stay" and leave him alone. Leaving the dog becomes a correction – all the fun ceases immediately if he does not pay attention. Do not add to his troubles by becoming irritated. Taking something away from your dog that he values– i.e. you yourself – is enough. The upshot will be that the contact between you and your dog will increase, and that the conflicts and irritations will decrease.

A time out only works if the dog really feels that he is losing something of value.

If the dog enjoys sitting around tied up, observing other dogs, then your time out will not work. Think about if your rewards really are considered as rewards by the dog! Maybe he will feel better if you skip his last meal before training, so that he becomes more food-motivated. And how is your own motivation?

Return when the dog is attentive and focused on you. How does he appear? His eyes should be begging you to continue working. If your dog shows his joy over your return, you can offer a reward.

SUMMARY

- An obedient dog makes and maintains contact – not vice versa.
- Reward the dog for initiating contact. It must pay off to show attention.
- Good contact is not about commands. Work in silence!
- Change speed and directions without warning in order to increase obedience.
- Foster a desire for closeness – offer something that is attractive to your dog.

On/Off
About environmental and relaxation training

Contents:

People who travel to southern latitudes are often amazed by the relaxed attitude of dogs running loose. These dogs lie about on the sidewalks; you have to walk around them. They do not move. They saunter about without a care. Their eyes seem to say: "You do your thing, I'll do mine." Some people claim this is the nature of dogs when they are allowed to roam free. That may be true, but I believe it is more the environment where they live that makes them "streetwise". My mother lives in Spain, and she tells me there are dogs that wait for the little green "walk" signal to appear before they cross the street. Quite simply, they have adapted to the environment they inhabit.

ENVIRONMENTAL AND RELAXATION TRAINING – AS IMPORTANT AS TRAINING WILLINGNESS TO FOLLOW

Life consists of many temptations. Some things will cease to attract us as we grow older and our interests change. Other things we see so often that we cease caring about them. For a dog, environmental training is about satisfying his curiosity and learning from the experience. He must be allowed to sniff, investigate, greet people and do everything else a curious dog does. Nevertheless, as time goes by the dog's interest will wane. Once he has had many experiences, very few things will excite him. Anyone familiar with dog shows knows that dogs will sleep for at least 24 hours after a show. The dogs may have remained relatively still, but all the stimuli at a show are overwhelming and exhausting.

Relaxation training complements environmental training

It's not always possible to give your dog a chance to calm down and relax. It's important that you and your dog learn to relax together in many different environments and situations. You must teach relaxation! This is an important complement to environmental training. Your dog should be able to lie down quietly a little bit away from you, or to be left home alone, or stay calm when you talk to your neighbor. He should be able to rest beside you when you sit down to read a book, talk on the phone, or visit with friends, both indoors and outdoors in different environments. Later in this chapter, I will describe how to teach your dog to stay passive.

Environmental and relaxation training – segments in teaching your dog to become willing to follow

Environmental training (or "socialization" as it is also labeled), and relaxation training are fundamental parts of basic training and very important parts of teaching your dog to become willing to follow. When you command the dog to rest, he should relax. When it is time to be active, it is you, not the dog, who interrupts the rest. He must be compliant while being active and while being passive. You need to flip the "On/Off switch", as I call it, to make the transition from relaxation to activity.

Reading suggestion: Read more about maintaining contact and training your dog to be willing to follow in the previous chapter.

Trixie shops with her nose

Both my dogs love new environments. They enjoy shopping almost as much as I do. Trixie and Stormy walk along the shelves, sniffing. I'm pretty sure their experience is a smorgasbord of scents. I follow them while smiling to myself. They allow me to enter their world! Sometimes it turns into a rather expensive excursion, like the time we went into a pet store. We wandered around the store, Trixie investigating the shelves, sniffing the bones and the other goodies. Nothing appealed to her, until we entered the gift shop next door. Suddenly Trixie stopped, raised her nose and inhaled a stuffed animal. This is what she wants! She proudly trotted out of the store with the toy in her mouth. The day's shopping was done.

ENVIRONMENTAL TRAINING CREATES CALM

"He is so calm indoors." This is a comment I hear frequently. But seriously: how often do you rest with your dog outdoors? Have you considered the importance of relaxing and being calm together with your dog in a variety of environments? How about sharing food, bird watching, playing with kids, and anything else that might tempt your dog to approach? How often do you stop during a walk to recreate the kind of mood you had while lounging on the couch?

Start environmental training early

Before four months of age, most puppies run around our feet. They tend not to venture out on their own. This behavior is necessary from an ethological perspective. If a puppy leaves his adult protector early on, he becomes an easy prey for predators. It is very important to accustom him to various environments during his puppyhood. Constantly taking a puppy to quiet places where every little change is dramatic does not help him grow up to become a calm adult.

Think about the movie *Crocodile Dundee* (1986). The leading character, crocodile hunter Mike Dundee, has never been outside the Australian outback, let alone in any kind of city. When he arrives in New York for the first time, he is simultaneously full of wonder and terror, and is fascinated by what he experiences. The later in life we venture out of our habitual environment, the bigger the adjustment will be.

Stormy goes to school

Safety and security are concepts often used in the world of dogs. Young puppies especially have an innate need for closeness. Without really planning to, I acquired a Labrador puppy a few years ago, and this created a bit of grief. How would I juggle this with all of the classes I had to teach?

Five weeks later, hurricane Stormy moved in. The next day I started a five-day competition-oriented class with six participants. I put up a metal pen in the classroom and lined it with a blanket. I also gave Stormy a bone to chew. There he could sleep together with Trixie, my seven-year-old Tervuren, while class activities went on around them. Now and then, I took him out, but only when he was calm and quiet. Stormy quickly learned it did not pay off to stand up and lean against the pen to get my attention. In addition, he learned to sleep despite everything going on around him. When he was not in the pen, I lugged him around in a cloth sling that I had fastened around my shoulders and waist. He lay there calm and safe when I was teaching, and also when I went for walks.

To begin with, I did not allow him to walk very far on his own paws. This way Trixie could still get her daily walks and activities, while Stormy watched the proceedings from his safe haven in my arms. Now and then, I would let him down so he could walk on his own for a while. Just like in the puppy pen, Stormy learned he would only be allowed on the ground when he was calm – and not otherwise. This presented many natural training opportunities during the week of obedience courses, and this strengthened the bond between us.

Choose the bus rather than the woods

A dog who becomes accustomed to a variety of environments and situations as a youngster has a head start. It makes it easier for him to tolerate distractions in his environment. He learns good manners – just by being there, without many cues. You may prefer walking in the woods to sitting on a bus, but an encounter with a person or other dog will take on abnormally large proportions in the woods compared to the bus. Make sure the puppy experiences a variety of environments. That is how he learns what is normal. Cafes and buses are perfect places for visiting, as long as you protect the puppy from being stepped on. He will feel at ease being near you, no matter where you are. Socializing a puppy early on avoids problems later on. Socialization by exposure to different environments will make the dog obedient and secure in your company.

Environmental training in several locations

Exposing your dog to different environments is easy. Take the bus instead of the car. Go to the nearest farmers' market and sit down for a cup of coffee and a muffin. Look at people together, split the muffin between you and then go home. By slowly strolling about in different environments, the dog will learn to accept what happens around him without acting out.
Additional environmental training...

- on city streets
- in traffic
- on trams and trains
- in the countryside
- in the woods
- near water
- among adults
- among children
- close to horses
- close to other dogs
- on training grounds

Think about:

What environments do you usually move around in with your dogs?
Where does your dog need to be in order to remain calm and feel safe?

Ella cannot sit still

Monica and Ella, her young mixed breed bitch, were students in one of my classes. The owner was clearly irritated at her dog, who just wanted to greet everyone she encountered. Monica jerked on the leash and commanded the dog to sit. The dog sat for about ten seconds, only to then continue lunging forward. Again, the aggravated owner pulled the puppy close. Monica believed that Ella was only interested in the environment and never cared for her. She never considered whether she offered her dog any kind of guidance and safety. As Ella had not had any kind of environmental or relaxation training as a puppy, either from the breeder or from Monica, she had problems dealing with different situations. Monica, on the other hand, communicated with the puppy using words that Ella did not understand. Instead, it would have been better to sit down with the dog and firmly, but kindly, explain to Ella she was not allowed to lunge on the leash when she greeted someone.

We started environmental training by asking Monica and Ella to take a bus ride. This forced Monica to stop shouting at Ella. Instead, she had to use her hands in a calm way to make Ella sit quietly between her knees. After a week of training, Ella was a lot calmer and Monica a lot quieter. When Ella did start getting restless, Monica sat down and stroked her on the chest with circular movements.

We tend to believe the dog should be able to sit quietly for a long time, just because we have told him to. However, just as we cannot expect a two-year old to sit quietly for any length of time, we cannot have unrealistic expectations of a young dog. When we do, it causes conflicts.

RESTING TOGETHER STRENGTHENS THE BONDS.

During my education with Anders Hallgren – a Swedish psychologist who has worked with both humans and dogs – I complained about all the dog walks I had to take. Anders replied that if I sat down on a tree stump and remained quiet, I would learn a lot about what goes on inside a dog's head. At that time, I didn't understand what he meant. Why do I have to keep walking the dogs when there is more important stuff to do? In his natural habitat, your dog might have slept, played, hunted and gone for walks. How many of those behaviors get an outlet during a walk?

Constantly being on the move without sitting down now and then to rest instills a bad habit: a dog who constantly pulls on the leash. In the end, it creates an increasingly independent dog. Thus, it is important that you teach your dog how to stay calm in different situations. Walking outdoors also means being able to stay still and rest together. With a young dog, it is most important to go for several, but short, walks and to switch between Sneak Away exercises, *(see the chapter on "Who follows whom? About contact and training willingness to follow)* mental activation and periods of rest. The cue for peace and quiet is quite simply your own body language and frame of mind. Go to a park, sit down on the ground and pull out some picnic food from your backpack. Lean against a tree and enjoy the peace. Resting together will strengthen the bond between you and your pooch!

Who decides how long you rest – you or the dog?

Like some people, some dogs are never satisfied. They always have to look around the corner to see if the grass is greener on the other side. Sometimes I sit in the woods chatting with an owner about his or her dog. Meanwhile, the dog walks around investigating the odors around us. Suddenly, the undergrowth changes. Instead of the tall grass where the dog has been sniffing around, there is now a footpath. The dog stops and starts sniffing the air, standing still, and looking hesitant for a moment. Then he makes a choice. After a quick glance our way, he steps over the path to see what is on the other side. Alternatively, he may turn his head and look at us, gaze across the path again – and then turn back.

I am the one who decides how long to rest, not the dog. When I start teaching, there should be no distractions in the form of other dogs or people. In some cases, it is enough for me to clear my throat or rapidly clap my hands to make the dog turn around quickly. Other times, I may need to throw a stick or something at the dog's behind. Then, when he makes and maintains contact with me, I talk to him in a low and friendly voice without making a big deal about what happened.

The next time you watch your dog stand there, faced with a choice, and he spontaneously turns back, you should use the same low voice and friendly voice for praise. This is how the dog learns to relax when you rest, without having to give him a command.

Is it time to go?

In one of my classes, the students had to study how their dogs react to how we stood up after a break. On the first occasion, the owner was to quietly stand up and leave. On another, he or she was to get up quickly and leave immediately. On a third occasion, he or she was to stand up slowly, do some stretches, and then quietly walk away.

One of the dogs in the group did not react much when the owner quietly stood up and left but followed in a disinterested way. On the second occasion, when the owner got up quickly and firmly left, the dog got up and followed just a few steps after. He looked scared, as if he suspected that the owner was heading towards danger. On the third occasion, when the owner got up, stretched and yawned, the dog responded actively by wagging his tail and stretching. Then, when the owner left, the dog followed attentively.

This example indicates how important the way we indicate it's time to go is. Our dogs often have a strong emotional reaction if we quickly wrap up our picnic lunch in the woods, get up from the couch when answering the phone, or when somebody rings the doorbell. Think about how you get up – what are you actually telling your dog?

RELAXATION TRAINING – A PREVENTIVE MEASURE

If the dog decides himself when to rest, there are seldom any problems. When we find ourselves in circumstances with more distractions, it might be a different story. A dog that never learns to relax may even increase his activity level when his humans relax. He whines and looks at us. He may run away and grab something – anything to get attention. A dog that has received relaxation and environmental training will just lie down and relax. Teaching relaxation thus becomes training as a preventive measure, and you become a facilitator, not a punisher. It makes it possible for the dog to take it easy when you want – and for as long as you want. You are the only one to decide when the fun starts again.

Fred behaving badly

Fred was a Schipperke who made his owners Charles and Caroline furious. He would run around and around in their apartment barking. There was never a moment of peace whenever Caroline and Charles had visitors. Fred jumped up and down on the sofa, trying to hump the visitors and standing in front of them barking. For there to be any kind of normal conversation, Caroline would have to spend the evening with Fred on her lap. The situation was, of course, insufferable and unsustainable. Confining Fred to another room was not an option as he would continue to bark up a storm and try his best to get out.

When Caroline and Charles came to see me, I asked them to let Fred lose. That unleashed a whirlwind. I let him be, curious as to who he was and what he would do next. Caroline and Charles were to stay quiet and ignore their dog, which ultimately made his behavior worse. He looked at us as if saying: "Come on, don't you see what I am up to, tell me what to do!"

After a while, I found that Fred was an active and smart dog who had successfully trained his family. I asked Caroline and Charles what they usually did when Fred threw a tantrum. They explained that they would usually play with him or take him for a walk so that he calmed down. The picture became clear. I called Fred over and showed him a treat. When he showed interest, I closed my hand around the treat and held my hand still on my knee. Fred immediately started his usual shenanigans. He threw himself on my hand, bit it, barked, backed up and behaved atrociously. He reminded me a lot of a two-year old who has discovered the candy shelf in the store and will do anything in this power to get what he wants. Finally, after several minutes, Fred briefly gave up and sat down. I immediately rewarded him by throwing him some treats. Fred flew up and ran after them. Then the whole circus began again. This is exactly what I wanted. Fred had to learn to get what he wanted by behaving in a calm and controlled way. After the first eight or ten times, he finally got it. Fred now tried sitting down when he came up to me.

At last, Caroline and Charles started to understand the behavior patterns they had created. Fred's bad behavior resulted in Caroline and Charles engaging him in different ways. They nagged Fred loudly to no effect and tried distracting him in a variety of ways. Sometimes they put on their coats and took him outside for a walk. It clearly paid off better for Fred to challenge Caroline and Charles rather than to behave like a good boy.

Caroline and Charles had to change their habits radically. The whole point was to play with Fred and take him outside only when he was calm. In some situations, where it was impossible to ignore his bad behaviors, I advised them to quietly, and without anger pour a bowl of water over him. When Caroline and Charles started rewarding Fred for correct behaviors, they prevented future bad behavior. It decreased the amount of discipline. Fred got their attention, he got his walks and play, but only when he behaved in a calm and controlled way, never when he behaved badly.

Training tips: The bone – video games for dogs

We do not always have time to train our dogs. Just like when we give kids a computer game or a video to keep them occupied, we can give the dog a bone to gnaw on when you just don't have time to train him. If you place the bone on the dog's bed, he will learn to stay in one place. The only place he is allowed to have his bone is in his bed.

HOW YOUR MOOD AFFECTS YOUR DOG

Environmental training and relaxation training presupposes a calm owner. Using a loud voice to the dog telling him to be calm and quiet is like screaming to the kids to go to sleep. What are we actually asking the dog? In spite of our own nervousness, irritation or worry, we require the dog to obey our commands and cues. Our words are hypocritical. Our body language and our moods tell the dog something else – get excited! Correcting an agitated dog may work temporarily. It is seldom a long-term solution. The permanent solution is instead to rest with the dog in different environments and situations. This is about setting limits as to when, how, and for how long we rest. A dog's education that lacks this component means nagging, correction, and irritation.

Lillian and Sluggo – like mother, like dog

Lillian and Sluggo rush through the door like a whirlwind. Sluggo, at the end of his leash, throws himself back and forth. Excitedly, Lillian sits down on a chair and commands Sluggo to sit. Sitting is exactly what he refuses to do. But no commands in the world can make a dog believe what we say, if we don't first learn how to control our own emotions. So I ask Lillian to sit down on the floor with Sluggo and stop communicating with words he won't listen to anyway "But he knows how to sit," Lillian replies. And I am sure he does, at home in a familiar environment, but not here in class.

Avoid eye contact when you teach relaxation

When the dog wants to ask for something, we usually want him to make eye contact. A side effect of this is that we simultaneously reinforce the dog's behavior. Have you noticed what happens if you always wait for your dog to make contact before you allow him to leave? The moment you give your permission the dog rushes away excitedly. The eye contact is important, certainly on walks and as well as during other activities and training. When you teach relaxation, you should avoid it.

Think about:

Are you aware of which cues you send your dog when you want to relax?

Are you able to laugh and roughhouse with your dog, only to rest quietly together just afterwards?

THE BACKPACK – A BASIC RELAXATION EXERCISE

"The backpack" is one of the basic relaxation exercises I teach in my classes. This is about you and your dog learning to relax, regardless of the situation or environment. When you read a book, talk to friends, or watch others with their dogs, you and your dog need to be able to take it easy. You need to learn how to be calm and quiet. Only then can changes take place. Relaxation will lead to activity!

- Start doing "the backpack" exercise in a quiet and relaxed environment. Sit on the floor or on a chair so that your feet form a "V". The dog should sit between your knees with his back against your belly. If you have a large dog or one that does not want to sit down, you can do the "Peace and quiet by your side" exercise instead (see below).

- You can entice the dog with a treat to make him get between your knees. Make a "U" movement with your hand and let the dog nibble on the treat. Maybe push your dog's rear down. Give him the rest of the treat as soon as he is in place between your knees. Avoid eye contact, since we are teaching relaxation.

- When you have positioned the dog correctly, put one hand under his chin and throw a new treat in front of him. If your dog throws himself forward to try to get the treat, immediately counter by squeezing the skin right under the chin. At the same time, guide the dog's head upwards. If you hold him further down on the chin or on the chest, you will make it easier for the dog to use his physical strength.

- Wait for the dog to stop struggling and relax instead. It does not matter whether he is standing or sitting. Be sure to stay quiet! It is up to the dog to figure out how he will get the treat. Getting annoyed or angry will seldom achieve the desired effect. As soon as the dog becomes calm and no longer pushes against your hand, say "go ahead!" and allow him to look for the treat.

- Repeat this exercise both inside and outside. Train the dog in a variety of settings to increase the difficulty. To begin with, say "go ahead" while holding a treat. This helps your dog understand he can leave you only if he is calm. Repeat the exercise with the help of treats as many times as it takes. Your dog should understand that relaxation results in something positive! Vary the reward a lot. For example, you can allow him off the leash, or a continuation of the walk. Introduce the dog to different distractions, too. If you are consistent in never allowing the dog to initiate getting up and leaving, then he will quickly learn to wait for your go-ahead.

Greetings follow calmness

The treat described in the above exercise is a simple distraction, but it makes a good foundation for larger distractions. What happens if you throw the treat to a friend, especially if your friend speaks nicely to your dog at the same time? This is an everyday situation that often occurs with a puppy. If you want people to be able to talk to your dog without him lunging forward, you need to teach him that relaxation is a prerequisite for greeting.

Allow a person to come up and talk to you. Hold the dog by the collar or on a short leash. Be just as careful as in the previous exercise. Say "go ahead" as soon as the dog ceases being active. Then vary the kind of distraction. Can your dog stay quiet when a family member runs by? Can someone play with a ball or rattle a bag of treats? Can your dog's best pal play with his mom in front of your dog?

Do not always permit the dog to say hello! Sometimes you can reward him by playing with him in a different direction. Your dog is not the only one being trained – you will teach yourself how to stay calm and friendly.

Extend the time gradually

To begin with, this kind of training is not about relaxation in the sense that your dog rests or falls asleep. In the beginning, your dog will learn to control himself at the prospect of a reward, activity or greeting. Resting will come naturally by training distractions, as the dog learns that diminished activity will result in rewards. Then extending the time the dog is passive will seldom be a problem when all of the other conditions have been met.

Peace and quiet by your side

This exercise is a variation of the "backpack". It is suitable for larger dogs, or when you are standing up.

- The dog should be on leash and stand close by your left or right side. Hold on to the leash, close to the collar. If the dog is strong, you may want to put the leash behind your back as well to get more support from your body. The point is that the dog won't be able to lunge forward.

-Throw out a treat. You dog will probably struggle forwards. Stand still and do not let your arm move as the dog jerks forward. Put the leash behind your back!

-Wait for the dog to stop. As soon as he has stopped pulling forward on his collar and remains calm, say "go ahead" and allow him to get the treats.

Willie refuses to have his nails clipped

I had a cute little Jack Russell terrier in a puppy class. Willie panicked as soon as anyone even whispered anything about cutting nails. We started by teaching him the "backpack" exercise. I sat down on the floor and taught him the techniques. It was not long before he understood to keep still between my legs in order to get the go-ahead. I stepped up the training by placing several treats on the floor in front of me so that I could easily reward him. I grabbed Willie's right front paw. He found that worrisome, and he tried to pull it away. I followed along with his movement but did not let go of his paw. The moment he stopped pulling his paw away and calmed down, I let go of his paw and gave him a treat. Then I repeated the exercise. Dogs will quickly learn to make associations. Willie understood that he could control me by being passive. Very soon, he became still as soon as I touched his paw.

The next step was for me to touch and tap his nails. He started out by trying to pull his paw away. Again, I followed his movement and let go only when Willie became calm. Then it was time for the most difficult challenge, the nail clipper. I grabbed his paw with one hand and the nail clipper with my other hand and felt the alarm in Willie's little body. He pulled away his paw, I went with him but did not let go. When Willie stopped pulling his paw away, I immediately let go and gave him a treat. I repeated the exercise until he was completely calm. The next step was to touch Willie's paw with the nail clipper.

Fifteen minutes later, I could cut his nails. Willie had learnt to work through his discomfort by becoming calm and passive. A strange side effect was that Willie trembled more when he sat between my legs, before I cut his nails, than when I grabbed his paw. Then he became completely calm. The following week I taught his owners how to do it at their home. A week later Willie felt quiet safe being handled.

Training tip: On/Off – relaxation training by play

Playing with the dog is a fun and effective way of drawing the line between activity and relaxation. Playing "zigzagging the glove" teaches you to control the dog's activity level. How to play this game is described in the chapter "Play – and tell me who you are".

Tied up, calm and silent

Many dogs bark when they are tied up. The following exercise is a mixture of contact training and relaxation training. It is also a good exercise for you. It teaches you to look for the correct behavior rather than faults and mistakes. The point is that the dog should understand how to make you come to him by being calm and silent, not by barking.

Silence results in rewards

Tie up your dog and stand or sit about two to three yards away. Do not stare at him. Your attitude should be calm and somewhat disinterested. Your dog will probably do several things: bark, sit, sniff the ground, stand still and stare at you, or maybe even lunge on the leash. He may even try biting the leash. If that is the case, a chain leash may be better.

When the dog stops jumping and barking, and finally stands still, reward by quickly throwing a couple of treats to him. When you have rewarded your dog a couple of times for standing quietly and looking at you, you can then wait for him to sit instead. Then start distracting him in various ways. Will your dog continue standing still and looking at you even when you talk to him? If he does, throw him some treats and untie him.

Now you can start introducing new distractions. Can you play a bit further away? Can you greet another person? Can you help train another dog? Consider the kind of situations where you really want your dog to behave quietly and attentively.

Tying up increases concentration

This exercise will be very effective if your dog sometimes has problems focusing for any length of time. It increases the dog's interest in being together with you by blocking the dog's free access to you. This makes it an effective tool in a variety of settings. Maybe your dog is always very interested in other dogs when you get to the training grounds. Start by tying the dog up and repeat the first steps. Then go up to your dog, untie him and work with him. Tie up your dog as soon as he loses focus. In this way, your dog will learn to focus on you.

SUMMARY

- Dogs that have received environmental and relaxation training are able to relax in many different situations.
- Environmental training and relaxation training the dog is as important as compliance.
- Your own attitude and mood have an impact on your dog. Are you able to relax?
- Teach the dog that relaxation results in activity. On/Off!
- Customize your environmental training to suit your lifestyle!

Play – and tell me who you are

Contents:

Play is an incredibly important part of canine communication. Playing with your dog is quite simply a way of communicating how important he is to you. The return on play is cooperation and friendship. This is well documented for both humans and for animals.

PLAY STRENGTHENS COOPERATION

Play is one of the areas in the human-canine relationship that is most laden with emotion. "He gets stressed when he plays"; "It gets to be too much"; and "I lose control" are common statements made when talking about play. However, there is no more effective way of entertaining your dog than actively playing with him. Play strengthens our confidence and improves communication. We learn to forgive and continue playing after mistakes are made; we learn to control ourselves and to respect rules to keep the game on track.

In my experience, owners who do not play with their dogs are also more standoffish. Play between humans and dogs establishes strong bonds between owner and pet. Thus it is not beneficial for the dog to play only with other dogs. Such dogs will probably become more fixated on other dogs than if the owner had also participated.

THERE ARE LIMITS IN PLAY

There is a lot of empty rhetoric about dog training. One consequence of this is that training may become too serious and demanding, and not have enough play and laughter. But the person who is able to play should also be able to signal when enough it enough. Play makes it possible to create boundaries between activity and relaxation. Are you able to laugh and roughhouse with your dog, only to rest quietly together just afterwards? Are you able to not only "turn on" your dog when you need to, but also "turn off" your dog?

Reading suggestion: Read more about teaching the dog how to switch between activity and relaxation in the chapter "On/Off! About environmental and relaxation training".

Rules are for safety

In play, we express many emotions: competitiveness when we run for the same ball, exhilaration while in close combat, satisfaction when we have outrun our competitors. However, play needs boundaries to minimize the risk of injuries and misunderstanding. In all kinds of team sports, there are clear rules for what is allowed and what is not.

It is well known that two play better than three, and this is true for both dogs and children. And arguments will start – just like between people – more frequently when the dogs are tired, or when one of them cannot make himself understood.

Interrupting frolicking dogs

Anyone who has had a puppy knows that in many cases it is next to impossible to interrupt a puppy playing with his friend. It does not matter what we do to distract them. The puppy would much rather follow the other dog and seems completely unaware of your presence.

If you want to interrupt play, try to avoid conflict and make demands that a puppy might not be mature enough to handle. In most cases, it is more effective to approach the puppy and give him a treat – demanding the puppy comes when called is too much at this stage. Rather, now and then interrupt the dog's play with goodies. In the long run this gives the puppy greater incentive to stop playing and come when called. Be careful that you allow the puppy to continue playing after he has had his treat so the interruption is not permanent. Otherwise your dog will associate being called with the end of the fun and games. Remember, that no treat in the world can replace play for puppies!

When you do interrupt the play for good, put a leash on the dog if you are not sure if he will follow. Give him some treats and interest him in a toy while you walk away from the other dog. The dog should get as much out of following as staying behind to play. Do not use the leash to pull the dog away from the fun. This will result in the dog running back to the fun as soon as the leash isn't handy.

CHASE GAMES – HOW DOGS PLAY TAG

When two dogs greet and accept each other, one will then often invite the other to play. He throws himself down with his from paws on the ground, retracts the corners of his mouth and pulls back his ears in order to invite the other dog to play. Often he will initiate a game of chase, meaning that the dogs play tag with each other, very much like children playing tag. Facial expressions and body language are very important in play, as everything is at high speed. The dogs will aim play bites at necks or legs, not backsides.

There are also surprises in these games of chase. One dog will hide behind a bush and suddenly pop out when the other one least expects it. They can sneak towards each other and pretend to be disinterested to trick the other. This is a game where both speed and imagination play a role. Herding dogs and sight hounds play these kinds of games to a greater extent than other breeds, as speed is a prerequisite for these chase games. Other types of dogs also play such games, but for shorter periods. In many breeds speed in itself is the enticement, and the dogs clearly relish being able to run away from others.

Trixie and Bella

During a walk with my friend Ingela, my Tervuren Trixie amused herself by trying to get Ingela's golden retriever Bella to chase her. Bella made some brave attempts at catching up with the nimble Trixie without much success. Instead, Bella tried to bump into Trixie as she was running past. That also failed. Laughter sparkled in Trixie's eyes when she elegantly eluded Bella with a rapid sprint in front of her nose.

Puppy's game can be misunderstood

"Mommy, Leo bit me. Stupid dog!" The children's howl when their new puppy hangs onto their pants has prompted many a desperate phone call to the breeder. What is wrong with the growling little beast? When it comes to chasing and biting, a little puppy often has no clue about what is and is not allowed. He does not understand that we do not share his interest in chase games, going for mops or running kids. Following and chasing rapid movements is stimulating for dogs. Children's rapid movements unconsciously invite pursuit.

Young dogs will play games of chase whether we want to or not. Be the one to take the initiative! Invite your dog to play when he moves towards you, not away from you, and redirect his interest away from your legs to an acceptable toy or a treat.

Interrupting unwanted chase games

When we don't feel like playing, it is usually enough to ignore the puppy, and at the same time avert our eyes. This is the signal that older dogs use to indicate a lack of interest. Loudly saying "No!", making large arm gestures and trying to pull the pants away from the dog will have the opposite effect. The same thing happens when we stare at the dog, push him away, or yell at him. In fact, those actions will increase the dog's interest in the behavior. If the dog becomes sufficiently agitated, he can become completely blind to what you want him to do as he hunts for hands and feet.

One way to interrupt an unwanted game of chase is to pretend to be wounded. Use body language that indicates sadness and pain. Many dogs will have a very strong reaction to this and moderate their behavior. Water is sometimes an excellent correction, as it has a surprise effect. Fill a plastic spray bottle with water, or bring a cup of water, and spray or pour it quickly over the dog's head. This will shut down unwanted chase games immediately.

An important basic rule: the greater the dog's intensity, the calmer and more deliberate your signals must be.

Reading suggestion: Read more about how you can influence you dog by your own moods in the chapter "On/Off! About environmental and relaxation training".

"ZIGZAGGING GLOVE" – A GAME TO FOSTER WILLINGNESS TO FOLLOW

In my classes, I usually recommend that students bring an old glove with a 3 foot string attached. They use the glove in a game of chase with their dogs without risking that their dogs biting their hands or pants by mistake. The dog seldom has difficulty pursuing a glove that zigzags across the ground. In addition, this becomes a fun game for both owners and dogs. Speak in an encouraging voice to get the dog to chase the glove. Use your imagination! Stop the glove for a minute, like a rabbit sitting there waiting. When the dog touches the glove with his nose, the rabbit/glove dashes off along the ground. It is not possible to persuade your dog that play is fun. The dog needs engagement and creativity to perceive an activity as play.

Play – and teach relaxation

Decide for yourself how intense your dog's play should be. Maybe you will interrupt the game precisely when your dog has caught the glove. Maybe you will roughhouse and play tug with it, pulling in the opposite direction. Also vary for how long you play. End the game by calmly grabbing your dog's collar and letting go of the toy at the same time. What emotion will help the dog understand that the game is over? Stand calmly and silently with the dog at your side. Wait until he lets go of the glove and continue standing there quietly without pulling on it. Give him the go ahead to continue the game and release his collar. Vary this by sitting down, keeping your hand on his collar or on the leash. What mood do you want to communicate? The toy is not so important just now, only your own ability to relax. You are going to play only when your dog is calm and quiet, without making eye contact. Maybe he will lie down on his side and ask for a belly rub.

Using this training technique, you teach the importance of switching between different moods and body language. You learn to control your dog's activity level by practicing relaxing together. Play makes the dog willing to follow – in activity as well as rest.

Training tip: Learn to put the pedal to the metal, learn to put the brakes on!

Switch between play and exercises that demand concentration from the dog, like sitting or lying down. This will create a stimulating balance between play and work. Learn to put the pedal to the metal, learn to put the brakes on – on/off!

When the dog refuses to grab hold

Do not try to coax somewhat cautious dog into seizing the glove. Try instead to activate your dog's curiosity. If you look at your dog too much instead of looking at the object, you may be signaling so much dominance with your gaze that the dog does not dare seize the object. Be content if your dog shows any kind of interest in following the zigzagging glove. Then quickly snatch it away, and immediately turn around and hide it. Then, when you bring out the glove again, wait until you notice that your dog has focused his attention on you. Take no notice of the dog. Talk to the toy, hold it in your hands and lift it towards your face, so your dog sees that you are talking to something – without him really seeing what it is. Drop the string with the glove as your dog becomes curious and approaches, and start the chasing game again. If your dog does not take hold of the glove within a few seconds, grab the glove again and "save" it from his jaws. Provided you act with encouragement and direct your interest towards the glove rather than the dog, it won't take too many times before your dog will be anxious to take hold of the glove before you have time to "save" it.

No treat in the world can replace play for puppies!

Ginza – a cautious lady

Ginza, an Irish setter, was cautious, even as a puppy. When she was a baby, she had had a powerful infection that delayed her growth. Ginza had no interest in play and could not handle demands. Taking hold of an old glove tied to a string and then roughhousing was not easy for her. Her owner Karin pulled the glove in a zigzag pattern on the ground. When Ginza seized it, Karin let her keep it. In order to increase her confidence, Ginza needed to feel she was fast and in charge. Karin sometimes crouched and sometimes ran after Ginza when she had captured the glove. This boosted Ginza's self-confidence and fostered cooperation between Karin and her dog, increasing Ginza's happiness and confidence. Karin then changed the game. Feigning indifference, she left, so that Ginza had to look for Karin to continue the game. She ran past and made a stand a couple of yards in front of Karin to get Karin to chase her. However, Karin turned and walked in the opposite direction. After doing this a few times, Ginza realized that it would not work to start the game by standing in front of her mom. She learned that the only time the game kept going was when she initiated contact with Karin from the side.

Let the dog figure out how to keep you in the game

How can the dog entice you to keep playing? Let him solve that problem himself. Maybe he will jump up on you to start the game again. Ignore him when he tries unwanted behaviors and instead respond to those behaviors you want to encourage. This is more efficient than responding to a dog sitting in front of you. Avoid "being fun" when your dog stands at a distance staring at you with an object in his mouth. Standing at a distance may create problems for teaching the "Come When Called" exercise. You could get a dog that halts some distance away from you to get a game going, instead of coming right up to you for play.

Reading suggestion: Read more about how you can influence your dog's behavior by rewarding him or ignoring him in the chapter "Become a better teacher – about learning theory".

THANK YOU! TEACHING YOUR DOG TO DROP IT

Never compete with your dog for an object. Instead, teach your dog that you like it when he carries objects, no matter what they are. This will be useful to you in future training. A dog who has been encouraged to carry stuff will be a dog who is easy to activate!

Frequently we worry the dog will destroy things or swallow something inappropriate. This makes us throw ourselves over the dog to grab the forbidden object away from him. No matter what he has taken, it might backfire if you get angry or afraid. Your dog may retreat out of reach, and your anger will discourage him from carrying anything in the future. There is also a risk your dog will start defending his stuff – your reaction will then cause a conflict. Instead, teach your dog to drop things on the ground or into your hand.

Nellie – a ball crazy boxer

Maud taught her happy boxer Nellie obedience and working dog sports. Mostly she avoided rewarding Nellie with play because she thought that Nellie would get out of control. Neither could Maud let go of the string with the ball. Then Nellie would dash around, jumping up and down in best boxer fashion, shaking her head sideways so she hit herself over the shoulders with the ball. Suddenly, she would stop and look at Maud. Her intention was clear – come on, Mom! Maud had unintentionally rewarded Nellie by trying to be a source of fun at the wrong time.

In every situation, there are always appropriate behaviors, but we often become so annoyed that it does not occur to us to cooperate with the dog instead. What did Nellie do right? She looked our way and came towards us. We started rewarding Nellie when she stopped and inquired: "Can we run now?" That's when we threw a fistful of treats to her, turned on our heels and walked away. After she had eaten the treats, Nellie grabbed her ball and dashed back past us. Again, we waited until she stopped and looked at us. Then we showered another rain of treats over her and turned on our heels. After a few times, Nellie no longer dashed past us but slowed down and tried to initiate contact. Occasionally she would let go of the ball. If we then walked a couple of paces towards the ball, this made her hurry to get in front of us and pick up the ball. We rewarded every interaction, no matter if she stood still or moved towards us and made eye contact.

After 15 minutes of training, Nellie walked beside us with the ball in her mouth, waiting for the rain of treats. Now we started saying "Thank you!" when we threw the treats. If she dropped the ball before the signal "Thank you!" we just continued walking and turned around in the opposite direction.

"I do not want to swap"

Some dogs refuse to exchange objects with treats. Often it works better to teach these dogs to drop the object on the cue "Thank you!" instead of giving it to us. Play with an object on a string. When you want to stop the game, pull the dog towards you using the string and then grab hold of his collar. Turn around, so that the dog ends up on either side. He is not allowed to stand in front of you. Stand calmly and silently. Wait for your dog to let go of the object in his mouth. If your dog tries to lie down, you continue to stand quietly.

As time goes by your dog will get tired of standing by your side and drop the object. The first time may take some time, but just wait him out.

The signal for dropping the object will be grabbing the collar and becoming passive yourself. When your dog drops the object you give him the go ahead and begin a new game or something else. Start giving the vocal cue "Thank you!" when your dog drops the object. Then teach the dog the correct association with the vocal cue instead of the opposite – locking his jaws around the object.

Reading suggestion: The exercise "Nice hands" teaches you more about how to use your hands way in training. Read more in the chapter "Here!" that is about coming when called.

FIGHTING CLUB – THE DOG'S WRESTLING MATCH

Most dogs play fighting games only when they trust each other. In a fighting game, dogs direct their bites towards the sides of the neck, the legs, and around each other's jaws. People who are not used to reading dog signals may interpret the growls and the raised lips as serious instead of play. But dogs that play are always relaxed in their signals. If you watch them carefully you will see them often showing the whites of their eyes. Turning away their gaze means they do not want to antagonize.

The difference between fighting and fetching

The word "fight" is completely taboo in certain circles. It is commonly associated with stress and aggression. On the flip side, some argue that fighting games are necessary for the dog to be able to burn off energy and focus for longer periods of time.

At one time, I was told never to play fighting games with my Labrador Nusse, as that could cause a retriever to develop a hard mouth and fracture birds and game in his mouth. I never listened to that suggestion. However, even today I am surprised that this perspective is still prevalent in the world of retrievers. I have never seen any tendency towards hard mouths when my retrievers carry game, in spite of them happily tearing and pulling a ball on a string. I am convinced dogs are intelligent enough to know the difference between balls they are allowed to play with and birds they are to retrieve. Other working dogs understand this. The working dog can distinguish between a wooden dumbbell he is not allowed to chew and a toy that he is permitted to roughhouse with.

Fight – and teach the dog to come

In my classes the students teach their dogs to approach them without commands. You can also do this by using objects to play with your dog. As soon as the dog starts pulling backwards, you drop the object. Back away from the dog and talk to him in a friendly and encouraging voice. Keep your hands on your knees so the dog learns to come all the way to you from the very beginning. Do not reach for him. Continue backing up, so that the dog must seek your hands in order for the game to continue. This is an exercise that can easily be taught on a leash. When you allow the dog to have the object, then make short, peppy jerks on the leash. Move backwards and use a happy voice, and this will encourage him to come to you. As a result, your dog will look to you for continued play whenever he wins. Use the phrase "Thank you!" when the game is over and offer a treat in exchange for the object.

Reading suggestion: There is more about making peppy jerks on the leash to encourage the dog to initiate contact in the chapter "Compliant on leash – about the art of teaching the dog to heel".

Is the fight play or competition?

It is important to distinguish between fighting as play and fighting as competition. Fighting as play can be anything from playfully bumping a dog away to having a wild tug of war with an object. The emphasis is on the object. Fighting as competition has nothing to do with play - it is a fight about control over the object. In the competitive fight, there will be a conflict over who controls the object. We sharpen our voice, stare at the dog and try to extract the object using force. It is always up to us humans to decide if the play is to turn into competition.

There is a common preconception about never allowing the dog to win the object in a fighting game. However, when we study a younger dog and an older dog playing, we see that the adult dog usually does not snatch the toy away, but allows the younger one to win. On the other hand, the adult dog will signal that the younger one is not allowed to grab the object to initiate a fighting game. The older dog usually does not express dominance in connection with the drop, but will do so only when the younger one tries to snatch the object.

Carrying objects can increase distance

In certain cases, objects may distract other dogs. Dogs that carry things in their mouth often do not get in close contact with other dogs. By carrying an object, they indicate that they are carrying prey in the mouth. Other dogs respect this and avoid contact. Thus, the way we play with our dogs becomes important, so that we do not send signals that increase the distance in the game. If we do, we may suddenly create competition over the object. In other cases, objects may be a calming force. A dog that is too rough with other dogs may calm down considerably if he is allowed to carry an object when together with other dogs.

Negative fighting about objects

Very often we snatch things from our dogs' mouth without considering the consequences of our behavior. If we constantly snatch objects from our dog's mouth, he will start believing it is unpleasant to carry things – especially when close to us. People have different attitudes and place different values on different objects. A dog can dribble with his toy, throw it up in the air, shake it and make us laugh. If a dog treats a pillow the same way, we have a very different reaction. We raise our voice, stare at the dog and walk quickly towards the dog to grab the object. If the dog backs away, this often results in a fight over the trophy. By our change in attitude, we have shown the dog that certain objects are more important to defend than others are. In the dog's mind, we should defend these objects intensively, sometimes aggressively. When the dog has taken the wrong object, we signal threat rather than cooperation. This is when it becomes easy to create a competitive situation.

Certain dogs are bred to have a strong awareness of prey, for example the burrowing dogs like terriers and dachshunds. Even with dogs who are interested in carrying things, like retrievers and spaniels, there is a risk that there will be a negative fight. If we signal worry and agitation when they have taken the "wrong" object, it will become easier for the dog to defend their prey with aggression. Our attitude towards the things the dog has in his mouth will decide if the dog will cooperate or compete. Your calm will result in cooperation; your agitation will create worry.

Fredrik and Quito

Fredrik brought his German shepherd Quito to competitive obedience training. At the beginning, the dog had great difficulty relinquishing his ball when Fredrik asked for it. After giving a couple of commands, Fredrik raised his voice. Sometimes Quito would drop it, but more often Fredrik had to wrest the ball out of his dog's jaw. I pointed out it was inappropriate to use force to get Quito to drop the ball. I suggested that Fredrik, rather than instigating conflict with Quito, would ask the dog to put the ball in front of his feet in exchange for a piece of hot dog.

Fighting is part of our human heritage. Fredrik was not particularly positive about "losing" this fight. He wanted Quinto to work with his method, not "bribe" Quinto into dropping the ball. My suggestions fell on deaf ears. A couple of weeks later, Fredrik was not able to take the ball from Quinto at all, and only then was he ready to change his mind.

As with so many other things, we have to change our own attitudes before we can change that of the dog. Stubbornness from both owner and dog easily results in conflict, which lessens the will to cooperate.

Play fighting with the intense dog

It is easy to overdo it with a dog that likes to play fight. He will constantly bring objects he puts down in front of our feet or in our lap, as an invitation to play. If we respond to the invitation too frequently, then the dog may become very demanding and pushy. He knows we will ultimately fall for it and start playing. Instead, pet and talk quietly to the dog when he brings the object. Perhaps exchange it for a treat, and then put it away. It is especially important for intense animals to use activities that create focus. Let the dog search for a toy instead of always fighting for it, so he gets some mental activation.

However, it is important that the human decides when to play, especially with a dog intent on fighting games. Do not stop playing with your fight-happy dog. Instead, play other types of games – such as chasing.

On the other hand, if we want to increase a dog's desire for fighting games, then we want to encourage his initiative. Play with the dog when he wants to show what he has found. Find the kind of play that suits YOUR dog!

Putting a stop to play fighting

Older dogs often initiate the end of play by first adopting a passive body posture and using an averted gaze to show that the game is over. They stand still in that position and may receive little bites on the neck while remaining still, until the younger one gives up. In addition, the older dog will often interrupt the play by suddenly finding an "interesting" scent. Sometimes I wonder if the scent patch really is as interesting as it seems, or if your dogs quite simply redirect their interest towards something neutral in order to get peace and quiet.

Try to learn from a wise older dog. Frequently it works fine just to sit quietly and passively, looking at something else, until the dog quits.

After greeting each other, some fighting breeds immediately start a game with bumps, pushes, and tackles. This kind of play-fighting may deteriorate into skirmishes when the game becomes too intense. Be prepared to interrupt the play before the dogs have worked themselves up into a situation, where they are too fatigued to perceive each other's signals. This is often similar to children's play that sometimes ends in tears when they play too hard.

Mother dogs will often interrupt games between their puppies that get too violent. Young dogs do not ever feel they are tired. Therefore it is never wrong to stop hotheaded games early on.

Reading suggestion: There is more about how to plan and use corrections in the chapter "Corrections – or revenge?" and about relaxation in the chapter "On/Off! About environmental and relaxation training".

Wiz loves to fight

Erik and Ingrid could not let Wiz, their two-year-old mixed breed (German shepherd and Newfoundland) off leash without him jumping up and biting Erik. Both of them felt that Wiz had an aggression problem. He would stand a couple of yards away and stare at Erik in a challenging way. Neither indifference nor aggression had any affect on Wiz' behavior. What had at one time started as an invitation to play by Wiz had now turned into a situation that Erik could no longer control. In my opinion, adult dogs that jump up and bite arms are often very social and not particularly independent. They do, however, love a fight, which means they enjoy fighting with us. Correcting this behavior by starting a fight with the dog is impossible, as that is exactly what he is looking for.

Erik's task was absolutely not to respond to Wiz in the same way. Instead of using threatening signals and yelling "NO!", he started rewarding contact. He threw a couple of treats to Wiz when the dog looked at him. Doing this took the edge off Wiz' attempts at provoking a fight. Within a week, his behavior had improved considerably. Food has a calming effect and changes the dog's motivation. Instead of fighting, the dog is redirected to begging behaviors. By responding to all of Wiz's challenges in a new way, Erik took control of the situation.

Do not allow others to play fighting games with your dog

Strange dogs seldom play fighting games with each other. There is no reason to allow other people to play indiscriminately with your dog. Even if the dog initiates play, visitors should not play either fighting games or chasing games with your dog.

It is much more preferable that you are the source of the positive parts of your relationship. Dogs will quickly turn their interest on people who are good at playing. If you try to stop the play, there is a risk that both the dog and the others will perceive you negatively. Playing is a great way of rewarding your dog, but it can also result in negative stress. Put away the toys so your guests are not tempted to roughhouse too hard with your playful dog.

AVOID TROUBLEMAKERS!

It is not unusual that dog owners claim their dogs just want to play, when in reality these dogs are looking for reasons to dominate or bully other dogs. This is easy to see. The dog has very stiff body language and tries to stay face to face with the other dog to make eye contact – and thus a fight. There are bullies even among dogs! Do not expose your dog to animals who love to start a conflict.

There are other reasons why play between dogs may turn into a scuffle. If this happens frequently, it indicates the dog has a low tolerance level. Play should not end in trouble. If you are the one with a dog that likes to bully others, take responsibility and protect others from his bullying. Training away a very dominant trait is often not possible. Neutering the dog may make life calmer both for himself and for others. In other cases the dog will have to stay on leash and be trained to be able to go for a walk and pass other dogs without showing aggression.

If you have a dog that up to now has always played nicely with other dogs without incident and then he suddenly starts reacting aggressively, it is time for a trip to the vet. Sometimes aggression may be due to pain, which the dog will associate with his canine compatriots.

SUMMARY:

- Play with your dog! This expands communication and strengthens the bonds between human and canine.
- Teach your dog the rules of the game. On/Off!
- Play with your dog yourself – if not, others will.
- Play outside!
- Laugh and have fun!

Become a better teacher – about learning theory

Contents:

From a historical point of view, dog training has been based on the notion that the dog should submit to our wishes. This was built around ideas that we have the right to demand loyalty, and that when the dog does not obey us, he is actually trying to "defy us" in order to gain standing in some dominance hierarchy.

Today, we know that both humans and animals learn a lot faster with positive reinforcement than training methods based on corrections and punishment. However, we do not automatically become nicer when we use positive reinforcement rather than correction to train dogs. The most important thing is actually our attitude towards training. Dogs are extremely sensitive to our moods. Nagging and frustration can damage a relationship more than just about anything else – no matter which method you use. When laughter dies, no amount of positive reinforcement will substitute for the joy of being together.

POSITIVE REINFORCEMENT INCREASES SELF CONFIDENCE

Positive reinforcement means we praise the dog for doing something right instead of building training around correcting wrong behaviors. Rewarding the dog for ignoring passersby, instead of taking this for granted, is an example of positive reinforcement.

As a method, training with positive reinforcement requires more involvement and planning than the classic correction-based training. Proper behaviors do not cause as many problems as improper behaviors do. They are not as "visible", and therefore they are easier to take for granted. In addition, many of us were brought up to think that individuals are shaped by prohibitions and corrections – not by praise.

Positive reinforcement creates individuals with self-confidence. They enjoy experimenting and learning new things – and they are not afraid of making mistakes. If you first correct your dog for a mistake, and then praise him for correct behavior, he will not have same sense of security and self-confidence as when he receives praise for the correct behavior *without* previous corrections.

Positive – and negative – reinforcement

For the most part, I work with positive reinforcement. However, this does not mean I never use negative reinforcement. Negative reinforcement means that the dog learns to do (or not to do) something in order to avoid something uncomfortable. For example, I teach young dogs they must keep quiet and calm in order to be released from my grasp. A dog will attempt various ways to gain freedom. When he calms down and stops struggling, then I will tell him go and give him his freedom.

GOOD REWARDS ARE THE FOUNDATION

In order for you to be able to shape and alter your dog's behavior, he must be motivated to work for a reward. Rewards can be the sound of your voice, petting, treats, and play – and much more. In principle anything that acts as an incentive for the dog to initiate contact with you – treats, toys, other dogs, people, odors etc. etc. – can be used to reward a behavior. Look around – the whole world is full of possible rewards!

Think about:

What is a reward for your dog? What is he willing to work for?

A reward – something the dog needs right now

A reward will work as long as the dog wants it. However, things that are rewards in your eyes may not be so in the eyes of the dog. My Tervuren Trixie loved being petted and cuddled. For another dog, petting may mean nothing. Dogs are individuals, just like their human counterparts.

Nor can we be sure the dog will be motivated by a reward in all situations and environments. What constitutes a reward in one situation may not be considered a reward in another. When the members of a soccer team barrage the guy who just made a goal with hugs and pats on the back, it works like positive reinforcement. In a different context, this type of joyful expression may be perceived as a direct challenge.

The situation determines what an acceptable reward is. A piece of dry dog food may work at home in the kitchen but certainly not on the kennel training grounds when surrounded by other dogs.

Do not take rewards for granted

Some dog owners grumble that their dogs prefer a certain type of reward to others. The reason is that we have stereotypically used the same kind of reward – or we have allowed the dog to choose. If the dog refuses to accept the reward we offer, he will teach us to give him what is most important to him. He will soon realize he can influence us when it comes to types of rewards.

It is entirely possible to teach the dog to perceive something as a reward, even if he previously has been indifferent towards it. For example, for a dog that does not like treats, don't always serve his food on the kitchen floor. Instead, hide his dinner! This will teach the dog to work for his meals. If you want to use play as a reward, play with your dog as a puppy. Otherwise, he won't have a need for play when he reaches maturity. Then he would rather seek out his four-legged friends.

The rewards are your tools. Sometimes you may have to refine them somewhat for them to work. And don't take them for granted!

USING REWARDS INEFFICIENTLY

Imagine that you are carrying a basket filled with food, toys, and experiences. What are you going to offer your dog from this basket? Surprise him! If you always give him the same reward, you run the risk your dog will refuse other kinds of rewards. They will not live up to his expectations. Teach the dog that rewards are changeable. One time you may pet him, other times you may play, or offer spoken praise. Sometimes your dog will get a treat; sometimes he will get to do fun exercises. It is also great to give one reward on top of another.

Sometimes even learned behaviors can function as rewards. For a dog who loves to bark, "Speak!" can be a reward when he comes quickly when called. Perhaps your dog likes to play Find It and hunt for toys and treats, or do a rollover when you tell him to. Try using these types of rewards instead of the usual petting or treats!

Vary your rewards

When we always reward the dog in the same way, he tends to forget what he is doing and instead focus on the reward. For example, when we teach the dog to sit straight by our left side, we will first offer a reward when he sits up straight. He will still learn to sit crooked. The reason is usually that we give the treat from our right hand. This creates an expectation in the dog that food always appears from that side. He will sit crooked to see better. Be very observant when you offer a reward! Routine rewards can create the wrong expectations in the dog – and therefore new and unwanted behaviors.

Different rewards have different results

Different types of rewards can have different results. Food, for example, is more calming than play. Verbal praise can both arouse and inhibit the dog, depending on how we use our voices and body language. If you want to teach your dog to be sensitive to our different moods and types of rewards, then you had better train yourself to use your whole being: whisper, make eye contact, pet, clap your hands, bump, run, rest and speak calmly. Try it all, and see how your dog reacts to your praise.

Internal and external rewards

Rewards can be internal or external. Internal rewards are rewards you give to the dog. External rewards are treats, toys or other stuff that you throw away or have placed ahead of time. The dog may take them when you tell him "go ahead". Other external rewards can be another dog, or an odor that you allow your dog to sniff.

One advantage of distinguishing between internal and external rewards is that you become conscious of the great variety of awards. It is easy to understand you can tell the dog "go ahead!" as a reward when the he sits quietly by his food bowl. However, every walk is full of possible external rewards, like other pooches, exciting odors and kids. For example, if you start regarding odors as possible rewards rather than problems, then you can turn a conflict over those smelly spots into fun training opportunities.

Sometimes it is easy to fall for the temptation and just follow a dog that lunges on the leash in order to sniff an odor or greet another dog. But if the dog successfully pulls you to his goal, he will learn that pulling hard on the leash is the key to success and reward. Then he will pull even harder when you don't want to follow him. Instead, teach the dog what he is supposed to do – not what he is not supposed to do! Anything the dog pulls towards can be an external reward.

The prerequisite for this is that you learn to differentiate between "Good" and "go ahead!" Read more about these cues later on in this chapter.

Gradual rewards

One efficient way to improve your dog's performance is to reward according to a scale. Sometimes your dog will somewhat indifferently lumber towards you when you call him, other times he will trot nicely. Occasionally, he will gallop directly towards you without interruption. If you give the same kind of reward regardless of performance, you will never teach your dog a rocket recall. On the contrary, you teach him he does not have to exert any effort to get his meatball. Instead, save the most highly valued reward for the best recall. Then the dog learns the more he exerts himself, the more he earns.

Withholding rewards – a type of correction

Withholding a reward is a type of correction. However, as opposed to the usual correction, where we add something unpleasant, here we withhold something the dog expects. For example, you can withhold a reward when you want to teach the dog to stop greeting people by jumping on them. Hold a treat about chest height and gently speak to the dog. If he jumps up to get the treat, hold it behind your back. As soon as the dog has all four paws on the floor, take out the treat and continue talking to him. When the dog no longer attempts to jump, lower the treat towards him. When the dog understands it does not pay off to jump, lower the treat even more. At the same time, continue to speak to him. If he jumps up again, quietly hide the treat behind your back again. Do not correct with your voice. You know the dog has understood the rule when you can pet him and talk to him without him jumping up. Another way is to turn your back towards the dog when he tries to jump on you. If he jumps, he won't be able to make contact with you.

Withholding rewards is a very useful technique at slightly more advanced levels of training. It temporarily interrupts the training. Imagine you want to teach your dog to quickly respond to "Sit". If he does not sit immediately, flash a treat, tease him a little with your voice, and then turn your back to the dog. The dog loses his expected reward when he does something "wrong".

As you turn away from the dog with the treat, he will often quickly run around and sit in front of you to continue the game. Repeat. Then the dog learns to try harder to get the treat. This is a very different training method than the conventional way that entails repeating the command and maybe correcting the dog into a sitting position.

Reading suggestion: More about withholding rewards in the chapter on "Correction – or revenge".

When can I stop giving rewards?

No matter what training method you use, you will never be able to take away the basic tools that maintain obedience and reinforce the connection between you and your dog. If the dog is used to obeying to avoid unpleasantness, you will probably have to repeat the leash jerks or establish dominance. The same thing is true when you work with positive reinforcement. Would you continue to give your best without ever being paid for it? If we stop rewarding a learned behavior, its frequency will decline. As time goes by, the behavior will disappear completely. Therefore, never quit rewarding your dog entirely, but vary what you give him, depending on his performance.

Training tip: Create prerequisites for good learning.

Always try to create the right conditions for learning. Make sure your dog is hungry when you have class. Train away from other students if you need peace and quiet. In most cases, it is possible to create the right prerequisites to ensure success for both you and your dog.

"GOOD" AND "GO AHEAD" – NOT THE SAME THING

"Good" is a word for praise, meaning "correct, go on doing what you're doing". You would probably never dream of saying "good" instead of "go ahead" before the dog jumps out of the car. However, praising your pooch at the same time as you throw a ball is very easy. Frequently and without thinking, we use praise as a synonym for releasing the dog. The dog comes when called, receives praise and a treat, and then promptly sprints away. Unconsciously and incorrectly, we teach the dog that he, rather than his owner, is the one who in charge of ending the interaction and the reward. However, do we really want praise to become an invitation to freedom? Do we want to risk that the dog misinterprets "good" as equal to "exercise finished"?

Sometimes I hear: "I cannot praise my dog, because then he loses his concentration." Of course, your dog can learn that calm praise means he should continue working and that excited praise means the exercise is finished. But it limits your training. You must constantly be aware of how you give praise, so that the dog does not misinterpret it. Teach the dog to concentrate and continue with the task independently of your tone of voice.

"Go ahead" – the cue to be free

"Go ahead" rewards the dog by giving him something that you throw, or have put out ahead of time, or anything else that can be found naturally in the environment. It means that this exercise is over – there is no need for the dog to continue the behavior, like staying or heeling, for which he was praised. "go ahead" is a cue for "free dog", while "good" means "continue working". These commands are two sides of the same coin. Both can function as rewards. However, by maintaining a distinction between "good" and "go ahead," you delineate your rewards – and help stay in control in the process.

Freedom to sniff – Cato's favorite reward

Charlotte and Cato, a Great Dane, were students in one of my puppy groups. The nine-month-old Cato was a difficult dog to motivate. Sure, he liked treats, and of course, he would run after a rag and roughhouse with his owner, but then his nose would lead him astray. I had Charlotte incorporate freedom to sniff into her reward toolbox. This allowed Cato to sniff to his heart's content after he exhibited the desired behavior. Charlotte began by training her dog in very short spurts of just a few minutes. Cato then received his reward – "go ahead" and freedom to sniff around for a while. In between, he had to actively focus on Charlotte. If Cato tried to put his nose down on the ground, Charlotte would quickly put her foot down on the spot he was smelling and indicate this was off limits. Cato learned that the greater his effort, the greater was the chance to go sniffing.

With a dog like Cato, we really have to examine the toolbox, as the usual rewards like treats, play, and social contact were insufficient. Quite simply, sniffing became a reward when Cato did something right. It was quite moving to see how he actively wagged his tail and sought contact with Charlotte in order to get her to tell him "go ahead". Even his play intensified when Cato understood he could take a break when he initiated contact. This was a "win-win" situation, where Cato learned it was fun to co-operate.

Teach "go ahead"

When I teach "go ahead", I keep the dog on leash. I sit down and throw a treat out of the dog's reach. He is allowed to stretch the leash to within about eight inches of the treat. Then I wait quietly for his spontaneous contact. For starters, a head movement towards me is enough for me to say "go ahead". If the dog understands this, I will increase the degree of difficulty and will not tell him "go ahead" until he makes eye contact. The point is to teach the dog to "ask permission" in order to receive the cue.

Then it's time to increase the level of difficulty. Turn around or stand up without paying any attention to the dog. Let the dog figure out how to get the treat by himself. Turn away your head or lower it towards your knees. When the dog softly bumps your head, then reward him with "go ahead".

This exercise will not only strengthen a sense of camaraderie and the dog's understanding of the command. The dog will also learn he has to become active to get his treat or toy. Let the dog continue pondering on how to get "go ahead" from you. When you change the exercise, the dog's obedience will increase and you will become more interesting. In the end, the significance of the rewards will decrease.
Continue training by petting and praising the dog. Continue giving the "go ahead" when the dog actively initiates contact and does not pull towards the waiting reward. You can use anything the dog desires as rewards: other dogs, people, odors, water, anything. The sky is the limit!

Training tip: Only train your dog when you are in a good mood

A dog arriving at the training club the first time will remember what happens. Other dogs, the instructor's attitude, and your mood will affect whether or not your dog has a positive or negative association with the activities. If you are irritated because your dog is the only one "making trouble", this will negatively influence his learning. Avoid training when you are irritated or unfocused. In everyday life, your dog is more tolerant of our irritation, but in a learning situation, the dog might refuse to cooperate at all. Only train when you are in a good mood!

WHAT – WHEN – HOW OFTEN – RECESS: THE BEDROCK OF TRAINING

To become a clear and effective teacher for your dog, you must know what to do, how to do it, and what the final results will look like.

Criterion – what to teach the dog?

When you are going to teach your dog a new exercise, start by breaking it down into as many parts as you can. Recalls do not consist of only the start, the cue, for example the word "here', and the end – there are many more parts. Which are you going to focus the training on? Do you want to teach your dog to spontaneously make and maintain contact with you in a particular environment or situation? If you do, then reward the dog as soon as he makes the slightest turn of his head in your direction. Don't wait until he starts moving towards you. The criterion for the reward is the first little turn of his head. When the dog starts exhibiting this behavior on his own, then alter the criterion. Now you might offer a reward when your dog starts moving towards you.

You can also reward a particular emotion in the dog. Imagine that you want your dog to sit quietly and attentively. If he nervously turns his head, then just wait quietly. Reward him when he sits quietly and looks attentive. The next criterion for rewards might be sitting quietly for increasingly longer periods of time.

Timing – when to reward?

Suppose you decide to teach your dog to look at you. Offer a reward every time the dog spontaneously turns his eyes towards you. After a couple of successful rewards, you might reward the dog when he looks away. If your timing is off, you will teach something different; in this case, it pays off to turn his head away from you. You have unintentionally rewarded two different behaviors. As a result, he won't ever learn exactly what he is supposed to do.

If you decide to reward your dog only when he immediately responds to being called, there is no point in waiting to give him his reward only when he reaches you. He hasn't had a chance to associate the reward with his immediate response to your cue. *In order for your dog to understand, the reward must occur at the exact same time as he does something right.* This is where a clicker is very helpful *(see below)*.

As soon as the dog begins to understand that first part, then let the rewards become unpredictable to keep the excitement going. This means we might occasionally throw the treat to the dog at the very moment he reacts to our cue. Other times we let the dog come all the way up to us before offering a reward.

Frequency – how often to reward?

During the learning phase, it is imperative that the dog receives positive reinforcement every time he correctly exhibits a behavior. After that, you can reward in a random fashion. The randomness makes it more exciting for the dog when he does not know which reward or activity he will receive – or even when. This is when the reward system works like a slot machine. Maybe we will win – but when, what and how much we do not know.

Recess – a passive part of learning

Just like when we cram for a test or solve a crossword puzzle, we need a recess – sometimes shorter and sometimes longer. Many owners of competition dogs will shelve an exercise for awhile, sometimes from frustration over not succeeding. A few weeks later, the dog might suddenly perform the exercise perfectly. We sometimes mistakenly believe that knowledge and execution will occur simultaneously with training. However, sometimes shorter training periods interrupted by another activity, like a walk, are more efficient. This gives the lesson a chance to sink in. The dog will then act immediately when he recognizes a situation.

The joy of learning is also important. Too many long training periods reduce motivation. It is always good to end on a positive note. But it's okay if you sometimes end a session because your dog cannot stay focused. Take a break rather than wait for a conflict. Sometimes, recess may mean a change of scenery, moving from one room to the next. In a learning situation, I sometimes throw treats down now and then. This gives my dog an opportunity to move around. Often a micro-break is enough for the dog to focus on the task again.

Training tip: Think, plan, train

Plan your training for the best results. An efficient way of prepare your training is to work according to the TPT model – think, plan, train!

Think: What do you want the final outcome to be? What are your training goals? Maybe you want to teach your dog to make spontaneous contact. What are the best training environments? Does your dog need to be off leash to learn obedience? How can you reward your dog?

Plan: How are you going to prepare your training? What behaviors are you going to reward? In what kind of situations/ environments will the dog exhibit the behavior naturally? Which rewards are suitable for each situation?

Train: Start training – and stick to your plan. If it doesn't work? Come up with a new plan.

TEACHING THE CUE

Make sure your dog understands what to do before you teach him which cue you are going to use. Otherwise, you will become a nag, repeating a command the dog does not yet understand. A good basic rule is to hold off teaching the cue until the dog exhibits the behavior. At the start, give the cue at the precise moment as the dog shows the behavior. Then, anticipate the behavior and try to give the cue a little earlier. Then you can see if the dog has associated the cue with his behavior.

If your dog lies down by himself, take the opportunity to tell him "Down". If your dog spontaneously runs towards you, tell him "here". When he was a puppy, my dog Mio amused himself by crawling. When I was nearby, I would say "crawl" and give him a treat.

TEACHING WITH SHAPING TECHNIQUES

Shaping involves gradually shaping the dog's behavior by rewarding small steps in the right direction. Ignore all unwanted behaviors. The dog will stop behaving in ways that are not rewarded. On the other hand, he will repeat behaviors we reward. This gradually shapes the final desired behavior.

The training game "Hot and cold"

Shaping techniques teach the dog to think on his own. He gets to be active and try out various behaviors to find out which ones we will reward. In the beginning, this can be quite difficult. Many dogs are used to being shown what to do. They have no experience of taking initiative on their own. However, as soon as the dog starts understanding the association between his own attempts and the rewards, a type of communication develops that I have not seen with any other type of learning method. Training becomes a game – with very strict rules. It works like the game of "hot and cold" where only one person knows the solution. The other person will gradually get closer to the target with the help of the words "hot" or "cold".

In the beginning, the dog is not very conscious of his own actions. His entire focus is on getting the treat. He may try shaking his paw or nibbling at your hand to get the treat. However, my experience is that the reward gradually becomes less important. The dog learns he can influence me by displaying certain behaviors. Who trains whom is hard to say when it comes to shaping techniques. The dog displays behaviors, and I reward responses that move towards the desired target.

Shaping develops your ability to read your dog

Working with shaping techniques is not very easy the first time, but this method actually develops your own ability to read your dog's signals. In addition, it will increase your awareness of the importance of correct timing. You will get exactly what you give! This means that incorrect timing will teach the dog something completely different than what you intended. The most common mistake we make in the beginning is not paying attention to small changes. Instead, we wait for behaviors that we consider to be "correct" – like lying down, sitting or standing. However, dogs do infinitely more than that. They turn their heads, lick their lips, move a paw, and wag their tails. Learn to observe simple behaviors before attempting to shape complex behaviors. For example, try to reward a spontaneous stop, spontaneous eye contact, spontaneous grabbing of an object, and spontaneous contact on our left side. After that, you can use shaping techniques to shape a more specific behavior, like only rewarding the dog when he stops immediately. Then ignore all other forms of halts.

Training tip: Train frequently but briefly

Time is of the essence in all learning. Train your dog frequently but keep it short. Few dogs are capable of focusing for more than a couple of minutes at a time. Then they need a break. A minute of rest might be all you need before training can resume.

Exercise for geniuses

Before you start training with shaping techniques, the dog must learn the rules for receiving the reward – namely to be active in spite of his owner remaining still. Sit on the floor with a treat in your hand and place your hand on top of your thigh. Make sure the dog can't shove your hand out of place. Don't do anything if the dog nibbles on your hand to get the treats. When he stops nibbling and pulls back his nose, reward him immediately by giving him the treat or throwing it on the ground. Continue to reward the dog as he pulls his nose away from the treat until he understands he must take a step back to get his reward. Now you have taught the dog it doesn't pay to try to steal the treat from your hand. He must actively display a particular behavior to get it!

Then I reward the slightest change in the dog's behavior, no matter what it is. Maybe he will turn his head, lick his chops, or lift a paw. I reward all kinds of behavior. Then the dog quickly learns I want him to initiate activity. Now that the dog understands the game is about influencing me, the training itself can start.

A minute of rest might be all you need before training can resume.

Susanne and Tess – learning Fetch by shaping

Susanne wanted to activate her dog by searching for and fetching objects. However, her Cairn terrier Tess was not particularly interested in objects, particularly not when there were interesting odors around. We started the training by tempting Tess with a treat. I said "thank you" at the same time she got her treat. I repeated this about ten times, until Tess reacted to "thank you" with positive expectations.

Then I took a cloth rag in my hand. At the exact moment when Tess looked at the rag, I said "thank you" and gave her a treat. After a couple of repetitions, Tess left and did her own thing for a while. Then she laid down to rest.

Sometimes it can be hard to judge just how long a dog is able to focus when he is learning something new. If the dog takes a break on his own, it will tell us how long this particular dog is able to focus. This knowledge is useful when we plan how to continue the training.

After a small recess, Tess got up and immediately came up to me and sniffed the rag. She got her "thank you" and her reward. After this, things quickly progressed. Now she understood what to do to get more treats. I moved my hand in different directions, so that Tess had to fight to find the rag. She had to search for it near me, and then further and further away and finally I held it behind my back.

Now I only rewarded her more intense attempts to get the rag. Weak attempts got no treat. First, she got very worried and stopped trying for a short while. Then she pushed her nose against the rag more forcefully and got her treat.

Again, Tess took a break. This time her rest was shorter. After just a couple of minutes, she stood by my side and insisted on continuing. She was not immediately interested in the rag, because I held it so high that she had to jump to reach it.

After we did this a few times, Tess learned she could make me give her the treat when she grabbed for the cloth. Now I delayed for a second or two before saying "thank you". Tess attempted to let go of the rag when she didn't immediately hear her cue, but then she grabbed it again. So I said "thank you" at this point and gave her a treat. Soon she held onto the rag and waited for my cue before she let go.

TEACHING WITH TRAINING LURES

Teaching with training lures means that in some way you show the dog what to do. If you want to teach your dog to sit, you can for example guide your dog by moving the treat backwards over his head until he sits down.

Gradually phase out your training lures

When we want to use a verbal command for a certain behavior, we need to have a plan right from the beginning about how to phase out the training lures. Try to imagine how the dog interprets the lures. Otherwise, the dog might mistake the training lure for the cue to perform a particular behavior. We believe the dog understands our verbal command when he really does not. The dog on the other hand expects help.

Quite often, the training lure becomes synonymous with the reward. This is another reason why it can be difficult to get rid of training lures. If you hold a treat in your hand to lure your dog into lying down, you should vary how you give the treat. The dog will then become more conscious of his behavior rather than fixating on the reward. For example, put a treat behind you ahead of time. When the dog lies down, either give a treat with your hand, throw it on the ground, or tell him "go ahead" and allow the dog to grab the treat that you had put out ahead of time.

Try to get rid of your training lures as soon as possible. Decrease them gradually or try to get rid of them completely. Wait calmly and silently to see if your dog exhibits the targeted behavior on his own without help. Quite often the dog will try to repeat those behaviors that previously paid off.

Polish your cues

A common problem that can arise when we use training lures as a lure is that the dog does not associate our verbal command with a particular behavior, such as "sit" and his hind end hitting the floor. To some extent, this may be due to us saying "good" instead of "sit" when he sits down. But your verbal praise is not very important in the early phases of learning. Often it distracts the dog more than it helps. In later training stages, you will of course be able to praise the dog.

Try to refine your cues as much as possible so your dog will learn faster. Stay silent and calm and focus on using the lure so that the dog follows the movement. Change your training and do not be satisfied that you have taught your cue in one situation. Teach the dog to understand a cue in at least ten different situations. This is what makes it possible for him to associate the command with one single behavior.

TEACHING BY CATCHING BEHAVIORS

Catching a behavior means you reward a behavior the dog exhibits spontaneously, a behavior that you might want him to do on cue later on. How many puppies will not learn to pee on command? We catch the behavior and say a particular word just as the puppy lowers himself. Another common behavior that we tend to catch is spontaneous eye contact. Exactly at that moment, we call the dog. This results in the dog consciously trying to make contact with his owner for some kind of reward. Catching natural behaviors can also be used as a step in teaching more complex behaviors, such as fetching. If the dog spontaneously picks up an object during a walk, you can catch that behavior. Then shape the sequence, specifically teaching your dog to carry the object and give it to you.

As a rule, we can catch any behaviors we want our dog to repeat.

Catching behaviors makes you more observant

My experience is that those dog owners who practice catching spontaneous behaviors in their dog become much better at reading the dog's language than those who use cues to prevent particular behaviors. It's easy to end up in situations of "finding mistakes" and in a "no" followed by "good". It is my conviction that we first need to learn to observe our dog's natural behaviors while remaining silent. What is the dog doing? Which behaviors do you want to reinforce? Sit down and try to observe and understand your dog without saying anything. We are much too convinced that verbal commands are the key to raising a dog. Therefore, we keep interrupting the dogs to stop behaviors – the next step is nagging.

THE CLICKER – A TRAINING TOOL

A clicker is a little plastic box, smaller than a matchbox. In the middle, there is a piece of metal. When you press the piece of metal with your thumb there is a sharp clicking sound. Training with the clicker presupposes that the dog associates the sound of the click with a reward, like a treat or play. Then we can use the clicker as a marker. "NOW is when you did it right!" We use the clicker to mark a behavior the dog displays or as an immediate reward for obeying your cue.

More and more people are discovering the advantages of using a clicker in training. Some believe the clicker is a magic wand. However, if you do not know enough learning theory, it will not work any better than the usual "good". The clicker is no better than the trainer who holds it. It is a tool, not a method.

The difference between the clicker and praise

The big difference between a clicker and saying "good" is that the clicker tells the dog that a reward is on the way. A "good" is not always followed by a treat or play. The clicker just marks the target behavior; it is not a reward in itself. The reward is what you give after the click. You may for example give praise or a treat or verbal praise and play. The advantage of the clicker is that you can mark the correct behavior to the hundredth of a second it appears. In addition, the clicker sound is always the same, while "good" may be said in many different ways. "Good" always entails more or less of an evaluation of the dog's performance. The dog is forced to make a social interpretation of the situation: how happy is Mom – really? We run the risk of making learning more difficult.

To achieve optimal learning, the dog must be totally focused on his own behavior. The less cluttered the learning conditions, the easier it becomes for the dog to understand what he is supposed to be learning. The second I press the clicker, I am working completely "technically" with learning – I "freeze" the picture I want the dog to remember. The social relationship is introduced when I give the dog his specific reward.

How do I use the clicker?

When you teach the dog to associate the clicker with a specific reward, you should work in complete silence. Start by clicking and give your dog a treat. Alternate this a bit by throwing the treat on the ground and clicking when the dog takes it. Train at different places, indoors and outdoors, and never more than a few minutes at a time. Keep repeating this until you notice that your dog immediately reacts to the clicker with an attentive gaze, ears up, and a happy tail. As soon as you get this, you can start using the clicker in your training.

Do not change the picture for the dog when you click

Suppose that you are training your dog to come quickly when called. Use the clicker as a reward. At the same time, move your arm as if you were reaching for the ball you would use to reward your dog. Why? The risk is that your dog will associate the clicker with your arm movement rather than his own speed. Without meaning to, you may actually be teaching your dog to focus on your arm rather than running fast. You may think you are training recalls, while instead your dog learns to focus on your body language. The result will be that the dog will run slower and slower because he keeps looking to see if your arm moves. Never change your body language the moment you click – regardless if you are walking, running or standing still. Only when your dog has heard the clicker is it time to change your own position and reward.

Clicking away Misty's fear

One advantage of clicker training is that the clicker allows you to train your dog without assistants. Misty was a collie bitch who was afraid of children. She growled and lunged if they came too close. When Misty was a puppy, a large group of children ran to her and frightened her. Her Mom Yvonne was naturally afraid that Misty would bite and was afraid to introduce her to kids. When Yvonne and Misty passed children, Yvonne reacted by changing her body language and shortening the leash. That told Misty: "Watch out, Mom is indicating danger!" Misty never lunged when Dad took her for a walk. Dad wasn't worried and did not experience the problem in the same way as Yvonne. We trained Misty using the clicker. In a way, I suppose that in Misty's case the training resulted in the dog understanding that Yvonne was not afraid of children and there was no longer any reason to protect her own.

We humans easily transfer our own emotions and fears to our dogs. Successful training sometimes has to do with how much a dog owner can change his or her own attitude.

We began by teaching Misty the meaning of the clicker. Then we found a children's day care center. The advantage with the daycare center was that the children were behind a fence so they could not run towards Misty. Every time a particularly strong children's yell was heard, we clicked and gave Misty a treat. It did not take long before the Collie turned expectantly towards her Mom when she heard a high-pitched yell. Yvonne continued the training herself for two weeks. She went to the daycare center daily for short training sessions. Then we met again to see how the training was going. Yvonne told me that now, as soon as she heard children in the distance, Misty turned towards Yvonne and wagged her tail. The fear of children had disappeared for both Yvonne and Misty, as long as they were at a certain distance.

Yvonne's next task was to introduce familiar children into her training. The children had to be calm and willing to follow instructions. They were to throw treats on the ground for Misty to then find. Most often, after a few minutes, they could even alternate petting with searching for treats.

TRAINING WITH DISTRACTIONS GENERALIZES KNOWLEDGE

Peter and Pluto learn obedience on the training grounds. Pluto does not have eyes for anybody but his Dad, but as soon as they leave the grounds, he starts pulling on the leash, barking at other dogs. Why did Pluto so drastically change his behavior and stop listening to Peter? If we always train in the same places, he will only learn to be obedient in specific situations rather than in a variety of environments. Young people in urban settings who don't have cars often have dogs who are usually obedient. Because they don't travel by car, their animals learn to obey in many different settings. Before I had a driver's license, I went by bus, subway or train. I was frequently accompanied by my Golden Retriever, my brother's German shepherd, and my mother's Labrador. There were no problems having them off leash. They were even more compliant when they were allowed to be off leash at my left side than when I had them on leash. Regardless of whom we encountered, there were never any problems.

Training with distractions fosters learning

Introducing distractions into training is a necessary part of all learning. The goal is for the dog to maintain learned behaviors regardless of the environment or situation – his knowledge must become generalized. Your dog should be able to do what he has learned, regardless of where you are and what is happening around you – people walking past, playing dogs, honking cars, etc. It doesn't matter how much we training we do at home in the backyard or on the club training grounds, it will never be enough. We must train our dogs in other settings as well. When the dog understands he has to perform a certain behavior regardless of the situation, he will learn.

Start distraction training early

Contrary to what many others believe, I think we need to teach dogs to cooperate in spite of distractions early on in the training process. A distraction does not need to come from outside or in the form of a new situation. It is enough to place the reward on the floor instead of giving it from your hand. The fact there is a treat beside him will be enough of a distraction for the dog in the beginning. At the same time, this will increase his knowledge and ability to concentrate. If the dog makes a mistake, quickly step on the treat. As soon as the dog behaves correctly, give him permission to take the treat.

External rewards are good distractions

We can use all the external rewards the dog wants as a distraction: family members, other dogs, treats, food, toys, dumbbells or odors. Working with external rewards not only creates a dog that can cope with a variety of settings, but also makes a clear distinction between praise and "go ahead". "Good" with some petting means "go on working"; and "go ahead" means that the dog can stop the contact with you and leave the classroom. This creates limits and security in the training. You decide when to ring the bell for recess.

Training tips: Hold training sessions in unexpected places

Hold training sessions with your dog in a variety places and in different settings – particularly when he least expects it.

Introduce distractions before distance and time training

As soon as the dog knows a certain exercise, we usually want him to be able to perform it for a longer time and further away. The dog should be able to sit for an increasingly longer amount of time, while we walk away. The dog should be able to heel for a longer time before he receives his reward, or he should be able to run further away to fetch a dumbbell.

Training for time and distance early on in the process will tend to make the dog insecure. Instead, work with distraction training. Then when you increase the distance, your dog already knows the rules. This means that you do not have to sneak away from the sitting dog, repeating ad nauseam "stay", "stay", "stay". The distraction training instead becomes a carrot for the dog: "I will show them what I can do." Training with distractions increases the dog's knowledge and self-confidence!

SUMMARY

- A good reward is something that the dog needs and really wants.
- Think carefully about what you will use as a reward, as well as when and how often you will offer it!
- Recess is as important as the training.
- Repeat exercises, but go for short training sessions.
- Distraction training the dog will help him generalize his knowledge in a variety of situations.

Meeting and greeting

Contents:

In the world of dogs, greeting rituals strengthen the bonds between individuals while conflicts create alienation. It's the same way between people. Who wants to socialize with troublemakers? When puppies want to greet an older dog, they approach by lowering their rears, putting their ears back and retracting the corners of the lips as they lick the other dog's labial corners. They say hello enthusiastically as it's a question of survival. He must be accepted in order to gain access to food.

How does this affect the human-canine relationship? It is much too common for us to ignore greeting rituals and instead focus on making our dogs heel or come when called. We usually don't wonder about the nature of our relationship to our animals. Nevertheless, training becomes much easier when our dog learns proper social mores to be fed.

BEGGING – A SURVIVAL BEHAVIOR

We often prioritize making the dog sit before he gets fed. We seldom encourage begging. But both greeting and begging are fundamental survival behaviors. They are essential for the dog if he is going to be included and partake of common food resources. We can use and build upon these instincts. Perhaps it is time to revalue begging behavior instead of discouraging it. Is it really more important to teach a puppy to sit by our side or in front of us to get a treat, rather than encouraging him to wag his tail when he is close to us? Perhaps we should instead ask ourselves: how do we want our dogs to beg to get access to food?

How does your dog beg?

Find this out by sitting down on the floor and eating something without looking at your dog. What does your dog do to get you to share your snack? An adult dog will probably sit, because that is the behavior we usually reward. Unfortunately, as they get older and more experienced, dogs lose some of the natural instincts they possess as youngsters. A puppy is most likely to try to steal the food out of your hand. If he is a little on the timid side, he might become passive. The fight-ready puppy will bark at you as he runs in circles. Turn your back on him and calmly continue to eat your food. Most likely, this pup will try the same behaviors one more time. Sooner or later he will try to get his share by using more ingratiating behaviors; wagging his tail, lowering his ears and giving you woeful eyes. Suddenly you will feel a wet tongue on your cheek! It is up to you to choose which begging behaviors you like! Dogs that are more active do well when rewarded for calm behaviors, while more cautious puppies can be allowed to be more forward and assertive.

Winnie and Mio

Many years ago, my brother had an older German shepherd bitch, Winnie, who was very dominant over other dogs. Neither my mother's dog nor my own older dog felt comfortable being close to her, as Winnie wanted to be in charge. When Winnie was eight years old, I bought a golden retriever puppy I named Mio. Mio and Winnie developed a special kind of love. Unlike the other dogs, Mio was never afraid of or threatened by Winnie.

Every time I parked my car and let Mio out, the following ensued: after the two dogs greeted each other, Winnie would pick up an object. It could be a minuscule stick, a rock or a ball. Then she would lay down with her treasure without touching it. Mio started circling around her wagging his tail in a low position, rear legs bent, almost as if he was going to sit down. Winnie lay down with her head still, her gaze a little averted and ears pointing straight out. Mio lay down on one shoulder and slowly approached the object. Now and then, after a look from Winnie, he would freeze, only to continue inching forward. Sometimes this game could go on for a couple of minutes, and one time it took twenty minutes. Every time the outcome was the same. Either Winnie got up and left without the object, or she allowed Mio to take it.

Think about it:

I often think of Winnie and Mio when I see puppies snatching treats and food. What can we learn from our wiser, older dogs? Teach the puppy to be calm and level-headed when saying hello? Can you make the dog covet your food using only gestures and facial expressions? Have you thought about your dog's body language when you hold food in your hands?

PRESERVE YOUR DOG'S NATURAL GREETING BEHAVIORS

When the puppies' sharp teeth come in, the weaning process begins. Because of the pain, the dam will no longer allow the puppies to nurse and starts correcting them when they try. Puppies learn very soon to prod and lick the corners of their mom's mouth to induce her to regurgitate half digested food for them.

Puppies continue this behavior even after they have left their dam. We humans will also be exposed to this behavior whether we want to or not. Some people are of the opinion that allowing puppies to lick our faces is unhygienic. Indeed, there may be more pleasant experiences than being overwhelmed with wild kisses right after your dog chews on something questionable. However, in my experience a dog who is allowed to sometimes lick our faces will be a happier and more secure dog than one who is always being corrected for this behavior. Licking is the dog's natural way of showing affection and affiliation.

Preserve greeting behavior

As humans, we would rather use our hands when we make contact with dogs, if for nothing else to hold them away from us. But if we begrudge facial contact with dogs, we miss out on the most essential social signal in the communication between man and dog.

When we do not permit the dog to lick our faces, we instead say hello with calming gestures and petting. This teaches dogs to associate petting, treats and toys with our hands. Their interest will therefore be focused there rather than our faces. Without meaning to, we train the dog to focus on our hands and on rustling, noisy pockets.

Later, when the puppy matures, he will not understand some signals from us, because we chose to select away a natural reward – namely allowing our dog to give mom and dad an affectionate lick.

WHO ENDS THE INTERACTION?

Have you noticed which one breaks away first when a puppy and an adult dog greet each other? If not, try to study your dog during encounters with younger animals. Quite often, it is the older dog who decides the greeting rites are complete. The older dog will show his disinterest by starting another activity or he may react passively and turn away his head. If the youngster becomes too active, the older dog may, for example, yawn and turn his head away and upwards, or growl, or bark or even lunge to prevent further contact.

Who ends the interaction – you or your dog?

Your dog approaches and gets his treat. You pet your dog – and he then promptly leaves. Does this sound familiar? When you let your dog end the interaction first, you unintentionally teach him to associate petting and praise with permission to leave you. Thus you commit an almost mortal sin. He will then find it difficult to focus for longer amounts of time without getting distracted by something else.

Think about it:

How do you and your dog end a greeting ceremony?
Who ends the interaction?

DON'T GRASP FOR YOUR DOG

People who use their hands to grasp and hold their dog as he approaches risk destroying the dog's desire for closeness. Do not reach for your dog with your hands. And do not bend forward with outstretched arms. Do not let your hand become a vulture's talon! If you grasp your dog with your hands he will react with passivity instead of wanting to say hello. In the worst case scenario, he will withdraw and avoid your presence.

A good rule is to make contact with your hands only when the dog is close to your body.

"The Spin" increases activity close to you.

If you want to increase how much time your dog spends close to you, you can use "The Spin". Crouch down and spin away from the dog. Do not hold on to the dog or grab him. Let the dog actively pursue you to initiate contact. The intensity of this behavior will be reinforced if you reward the dog by allowing him to take a treat from your mouth. If your dog is a little further away, then move away from him and do not crouch until he is within arm's reach. Reward the dog for approaching and making close contact – not when he is sitting passively in front of you or keeps looking at something else. When your dog feels the same positive emotion for the "spin" as for greetings, you are doing very well.

Jerking and pulling worries your dog

There is usually a connection between hands and dogs that bite. Correcting, jerking and pulling on the dog with your hands will cause him to mistrust our hands. He becomes worried when close to us. Dogs that will not come close when called often have had negative experiences from being grabbed and held. Dogs that first learn to look up at our face and make eye contact before we pet them will seldom bite.

Reading suggestion: In the chapter "Here!", you can read more about how to teach your dog about making positive associations with your hands.

NO-JUMP GREETING

Puppies and adult dogs often jump up on us in order to get as close to our face as possible. When we shove the dog away and then crouch down, the dog often keeps jumping. The dog learns he must first jump before we crouch down to his level.

Instead, turn away from the jumping dog. When the dog has calmed down and does not jump any more, then crouch down and pet him. If the dog is very intense and eager to say hello, do something else for while. Do not look at the dog until he has calmed down and only then greet him.

It helps to have treats during a greeting. Treats have a calming effect and can distract him. This is a very fast way to teach a dog not to jump. It also helps when everyone in the family does the same thing.

TAKE IT EASY WITH FEARFUL DOGS

When greeting a fearful dog, it is important to take it easy. Do not stare at the dog, but remain calm and unobtrusive. Avoid quick steps and big gestures and do not speak in a loud voice. Do not talk to the dog! Instead talk to the owner and now and then throw a treat to the dog. Do not attempt to grab the dog. A dog that is afraid has no need for social contact, as he does not trust you. Instead, build trust by building on the dog's needs. These needs will vary between individuals. If a dog prefers toys to treats, you can throw a ball and then have the dog search for it. Work on the actual encounter between human and canine! To begin with, do not expect the dog to stay around very long. There is no need to stand still while training. Any situation will be less tense if you go for a walk together.

Have you noticed which one breaks away first when a puppy and an adult dog greet each other?

Expand your training

Then expand the training by withholding activities or treats. Hopefully, the dog will try to get his treat or game by initiating contact. Reward the dog initially for making contact. When the dog has started to trust you, it is up to you to choose when to activate him. Otherwise it is easy to create too high expectations. Once you have advanced this far, there is usually no problem reaching for the dog as he approaches you.

You can also walk away without paying any attention to the dog. If he follows you, start an activity a little further away so the dog feels he can trust you. Following you results in a fun game! There are dogs who get too excited by ball games, and you should hide the ball from these dogs so the dog can search for it. Alternatively, throw some treats on the ground for the dog to find.

Molly does not want to risk a greeting

The first time I met Molly, a bearded collie, she did not want to come and say hello. Instead she ran around in circles, barking at me. Her mom Christina tried coaxing her and using a sweet voice to get her come up to us. She wanted me to crouch and give Molly a treat to convince the dog that I did not pose a threat. I did as Christina suggested. Molly approached cautiously, snapped up the treat and continued running around barking. It was obvious that Molly did not feel secure in the role she was to play in greeting new people. Christina did not provide the kind of security that Molly needed. We decided to take no notice of Molly during the encounter itself. The only thing Christina was advised to do was to tell Molly to lie down and stay. Molly thus had clear rules to follow and no expectations she could not meet. Molly gradually started to calm down. Not having to greet made her feel secure.

In order to pique Molly's curiosity, I brought a bag of treats. I nonchalantly threw some goodies that she could scavenge. When Molly found them, she returned quietly. I threw some more goodies and Molly quickly went after them. This created several positive interactions between me and Molly – encounters that did not last long and that did not entail any social demands. Every time I threw a treat I turned my back to her so she had to walk around me and look for me from the front. Next I started walking after having thrown the treat. Then she had to run to catch up with me, and I chatted with her for a while before throwing the next treat.

SUMMARY

- Greetings strengthen the human-canine bond, conflicts alienate.
- Preserve the way your dog naturally greets. Reward happy tail wags and reward affectionate licks.
- You – not the dog – should be the one to end an interaction.
- Do not grasp the dog with your hands – that will decrease his desire to be close.
- Fearful dogs do not want social contact. Find out what the dog likes before you say hello.

Tattling is terrific!

Contents:

You are out walking your dog. Suddenly, he catches sight of something and stops. What do you do? A spontaneous reaction is often to say "no" when the dog stops and stares at something. But he is doing something right! Your dog is reporting he has seen something – or "tattling" about what he's just noticed. Isn't that exactly what we want – for the dog to stop and tell you what's going on? Why not reward this behavior? Teach your dog to tattle!

A DOG WHO TATTLES HAS A JOB TO DO

A dog who tattles will stop on his own accord and make contact with me – without my command – when a dog, a person, a rabbit or something else suddenly appears. The dog, person, or rabbit is the cue to stop or come back.

How dogs tattle varies a great deal. A dog for whom eye contact is easy will probably tattle by stopping and seeking eye contact with you. Some other dog will tattle by stopping and "pointing".

Tattling – good activation

When you have a dog who tattles, you do not constantly have to scan your surroundings to spot something that might suddenly appear. The dog it is your eyes and ears! Teaching your dog to tattle is a good form of activation. In addition, your walks will become quieter, happier and calmer, because the dog has a job to do.

You can teach your dog to tattle about almost anything – wild game, other people, bicycles, cars or other dogs. Around New Year's my dogs tattle about fireworks. This makes it possible to turn something unpleasant into an opportunity to reward them or play a game. Even other sounds, such as barking, shots or screaming children, can be a subject for tattling. As one of my students put it: "This is the ultimate in tattling. My dog started tattling about air planes!"

Ginza tattles about cars

My Labrador was much more interested in hanging out with his canine buddies than my Tervuren was. Thus, it was obvious from the start that I needed to teach him to tattle about both people and animals. Even a dog's best buddies tattle. It is a delight to go for a walk with two Belgians, a German shepherd and a Labrador without a whole lot of commotion. We two-legged beings can walk quietly and chat about everything and anything. When the need arises, the dog will come up to report that there is a new dog in the area. Pia, the owner of the other dogs, told me that her Belgian sheepdog, Ginza, returned one day at full speed, begging for treats. At first Pia couldn't understand what Ginza was tattling about, but then she discovered a highway further on. Ginza is not trained to tattle about cars, but when all else failed, they would do. A textbook case of the power of the ability to form associations!

Tattling must pay off

The training for tattling is built around rewards. A dog who tattles will scan the environment, not looking for something he can run towards but so that his tattling will lead to a reward – treats, a game or another activity. The expectation of rewards makes the dog turn and come back. Good rewards like food, fun activation, or play are prerequisites for us to teach our dogs to tattle. In the long run you can give the dog a "go ahead," when he has done something correct – tattling by making contact gives him permission to run up and greet you.

Training tip:

Do not try to teach tattling to timid dogs that tend to withdraw. These dogs need to learn to make contact with others.

Trixie's hunt

I bought my Tervuren Trixie when she was two years old. Like many Belgian herding dogs, she loved chasing wild game. Once she actually disappeared to hunt for a day and a half! So she was well "seasoned" for hunting. My first step was to teach her the sound of a clicker. Then we went for our first walk with the goal of teaching Trixie to stop chasing wild game. She was on her flexi-leash so I could control the situation. Very soon, a scent on the ground caught her interest. She moved in short zigzags with a rapidly wagging tail. I clicked the moment I saw this behavior. Trixie turned around at once. At that moment, I threw her favorite ball as far behind me as the leash would allow. Every time Trixie indicated a scent of wild game during the walk, I rewarded her behavior. Yes, I intended to reward her reactions to the scent of wild game.

The next day I again rewarded Trixie when she hunted for scents of wild game. The training was already having an effect. She turned around on her own accord and looked at me when she discovered a game scent. I rewarded her contact by clicking and throwing the ball backwards. Now she got it. Trixie responded by immediately making contact with me as soon as she found any scent of wild game. I could now start delaying the reward so she started moving towards me before I clicked.

Instead of the flexi-leash, I got a long line that increased the distance between Trixie and me. This did not affect her behavior, but she continued tattling about her game scents. I then cut the line about a yard each day. The deer had disappeared, so I had to trust train her using only scents. The critical day arrived when I cut the whole line, and Trixie was completely off leash. Suddenly, a deer ran across the gravel road. Trixie threw herself around in the air and galloped back towards me. Bingo!

Learning to tattle did not take away Trixie' desire to hunt, but it did create a new role for her in the woods. The wild game scents became a cue for Trixie to tattle about them to me, a role founded on teamwork and one that allowed me to control Trixie's chasing and hunting.

Reading suggestion: Read more about conflicts over hunting in the chapter "When problems are a fact – turning conflict into control".

Tattle training serves as a preventive measure

Teaching your dog to tattle is preventative training. How far it goes depends on you, the dog's personality and his interest in your rewards. Ideally, the dog would be ball crazy. Then he'll be willing to do anything o be able to play ball for a short time.

On the other hand, if you have a very independent dog who is interested in either balls or food, or if he is an established hunting dog, then you might as well realize that your dog is not going to tattle about everything.

TATTLING – CALMER THAN RECALLS

One of the most fundamental things we want to teach a puppy is to come when called. A good recall is the foundation of most things, right? However, if we believe that a solid recall is the solution to every problem, then we forget one thing: recalls involve action, not prevention. If we use the recall to prevent the dog from running away, then he has already done something we didn't want him to. The dog has already run away. Aren't a "no" and a recall cue in this case just two sides of the same coin? Both cues are fundamentally intended to interrupt an unwanted behavior.

Tattling results in calmer encounters

If we have a dog that knows how to tattle, encounters will become calmer and safer, both for the dog, for us, and for those we meet. Tattle-trained dogs are often less aggressive vis-a-vis the environment, as the tattle cue is a positive charge for them. Our usual recall cue may be full of aggression or fear, when we try to make a dog turn around when he has found something – these emotions can negatively impact a dog's encounter with others.

TEACH THE DOG TO TATTLE: REINFORCE THE BEHAVIOR?

Tattle training is built on rewards. This means that we start training the dog to tattle about simple things and we do not immediately expect him to be able to tattle about suddenly appearing rabbits. Waving a ball or treats in that situation is often doomed to failure. So start tattle training with the still young dog.

Reinforce the right behavior

One way to teach the dog to tell is to *reinforce the right behavior*. This means that you start when the dog himself displays the right behavior. Puppies, for instance, will almost always stop suddenly when they catch sight of something in the distance. They seldom have enough courage to approach the object. Even adult dogs often stop spontaneously when they see something that catches their interest. We correct our dogs far too many times in this situation instead of rewarding this behavior.

Teaching the dog to tattle when you are out for a walk is easy. The dog receives his reward when he *spontaneously stops* in different situations and environments, regardless of whether he is on or off leash. It doesn't matter why the dog stops, if he looks at you, or stops because something farther away has caught his interest. Tattling is really only a further development of basic contact training. The difference is that the dog's eye contact or stopping happens due to a sudden, external event.

A clicker has the best results

Using a clicker will give you the quickest and most effective results. You could also try using another positive sound, such as a squeaky ball. Even praise works well, provided it has a positive value for your dog. When the dog suddenly stops spontaneously, click and reward him by throwing something yummy or fun to him. Then teach him to stop and stay in the same place.

You can also give him the reward out of your hand. The dog will then stop, turn, and come back to you. If you throw something to the left or to the right, your dog will move towards the thrown treat. This can be an advantage when you are walking along a road. If you consistently reward your dog by throwing treats in the ditch, the dog will move away from the road into the ditch at the same time as he is tattling.

You can also tell him "go ahead." This means you allow the dog to go ahead to whatever he was tattling about. Vary the tattle training so it sometimes results in an activity that the dog enjoys.

TEACH THE DOG TO TATTLE: DEVELOP CONTACT EXERCISES

You can also teach the dog to tattle by starting from the usual contact training, where the dog stands or sits in front of you and looks at you to get his reward.

1. Stand still with the dog on leash in front of you. Show that you have what the dog wants and then hide it behind your back. Wait for the dog to make eye contact. Now give him the reward!

2. At the exact moment when your dog makes contact, have a training partner suddenly say "Hi there!" so that the dog breaks his connection with you. Your dog gets a reward when he looks at the person who is greeting him – *without* moving towards him/her – and then immediately returns to eye contact with you. Praise and reward your dog at the same time as you turn from the other person and walk away. This trains your dog to leave whatever he has told you about and to follow you instead. If your dog starts moving towards the other person, quietly tighten the leash to keep him out of reach. Your training partner will immediately assume a neutral posture. There is no reward in this case, but show the dog what he missed out on. Repeat the whole exercise quietly and calmly from the beginning. Work in total silence. *The cue* for your dog to make contact with you should only be the other person's verbal greeting.

3. Vary how you reward him. Praise with your voice, but wait a moment before you start playing or giving treats. If you always reward quickly with treats when the dog moves his gaze between distractions and you, it will ultimately seem like he is watching a ping pong match. We did say that the criterion for the reward is that the dog first focuses on the distraction and then immediately looks back at you. If you offer him a reward too quickly, the dog will immediately tell you the same thing again.

MAKE UP A TATTLE SCALE

When the dog knows the fundamental exercises, it is time to vary the distractions that the dog is supposed to tell you about. Make up a tattle scale! Start with the easiest distractions first. Friends or family members can help. Every fourth time you should deliberately add a distraction you know is too difficult. Your dog will learn the consequences of mistakes more quickly. If he moves away from you towards the distraction, there will be no reward. Tattling is the only way to get what he wants!

1. Short sounds like "hi" or "good dog" are the simplest form of distraction, and the same goes for rattling a bag of treats or a toy in your pocket. The distraction should be something your dog really wants. The person making the distractions should remain still.

2. Now it's time to introduce motion. The person making the distractions will move or jog past. He could also be someone who limps, or someone passing by you and your dog. The motion can even come from another dog. If this is your dog's best buddy, it will be really good to reward him with "go ahead", provided that your dog tattles without taking one step away from you.

3. Use surprise distractions. Have a person suddenly appear from behind a house, run past, and yell, "Hi there!"

Training tip: A variety of rewards make training exciting

As soon as the dog understands what tattling is about, you can start changing your rewards. Reward him sometimes with "good", sometimes give him a treat, a game, or some other activity. Not knowing what reward is coming your way makes the training more exciting!

Reading suggestion: Read more about how to vary rewards in the chapter "Become a better teacher – about learning theory".

CONTINUE TRAINING WITH NATURAL DISTRACTIONS

When the dog understands the basic exercises, it is time to continue training with "natural" distractions. For starters, you will have to keep an eye out for what your dog is going to tell you about. When you see a tattle-worthy object, stop at an appropriate distance and show your dog something he wants. Then hide the reward behind your back. Hopefully, your dog will recognize the situation and start looking for something, only to then turn towards you and tell you about it. Now the dog will start developing into a first class tattletale!

When the dog knows how to tattle when you stand still, repeat the training while moving. Avoid your dog tattling by your left side in heel position if you and your dog also participate in obedience competitions. Tattling is everyday training.

The better the report, the better the reward

When the dog understands you want him to tell you about a variety of things, you should on occasion only reward him with verbal praise. Save the best prizes for encounters with wild game, joggers, bicyclists, and other dogs. Vary the rewards – but never stop giving them altogether. Why else would your dog tattle?

Think about:

What distracts your dog? What would you really like him to tell you about?

SUMMARY:

- A dog who tattles stops automatically and makes contact, when something suddenly appears.
- Tattling is a great way to activate. It gives the dog a job!
- Tattle training makes for calmer and safer walks.
- Tattling must pay off! Your dog will tattle to get paid.
- The better the report, the better the reward.

Loose leash walking – teaching your dog good leash etiquette

Contents:

Leash training can be a nightmare or as easy as it gets. Some dogs have more difficulty than others when learning to walk calmly on a leash. These may be dogs with an active temperament and spring-loaded legs, or dogs that are under-stimulated physically and mentally, or dogs that find it unpleasant to walk with a frustrated and grumpy owner. How much fun can that be?

I generally console people with the fact that many owners who compete at the highest level often fail to teach their dogs to walk calmly on a leash in everyday situations. The "heel" command, after which the dog should line up with your left leg, close beside you, are very clear cues to the dog about what to do in competition or training. There is no such obvious cue, however, during your everyday walk when the dog's "only" responsibility is not to pull on the leash.

TRAIN THE DOG TO BE WILLING TO FOLLOW ON LEASH

Leash training is not about what to do when the dog pulls on the leash. Rather it is about how you should conduct yourself so the dog will understand that walking is a joint activity – and that you are the leader. Teaching the dog how to be willing to follow on a leash is not much different than teaching him how to behave on a leash.

Use body language

To successfully teach your dog to walk properly on a leash, you must examine your own behavior. Stop talking and stop nagging. Nobody – humans or animals – likes to be nagged! In addition, nagging reduces your dog's desire to cooperate. Rather than using words, use your body language to show what you mean. Your dog understands you better. This is similar to teaching off-leash obedience, such as changing directions and pace. Watch how your dog behaves on leash and imitate his behavior: stop, change direction and speed so frequently that the dog learns that you decide the pace.

Frequently stop to change pace. When your dog starts picking up the pace, refuse to follow. Stop suddenly at the exact moment *when the dog increases his pace*, not when he already hit the end of the leash. Then it's too late! The dog should immediately respond to your stop, before the leash is tight, in order to get a reward. At that point, pile on loads of praise, cuddles, play, or let the dog run free. The reward is especially important if conflicts with your dog have been long-term. In that case, it's not enough just to change how you walk. If you neglect rewarding the dog when he does something right, he won't learn anything. To increase the dog's proximity to you when he correctly performs an activity, make a 180-degree turn to the right. Reward him with treats or play.

Reading suggestion: Read about contact and obedience training in chapter 1. More about the right turn can be found in "Close to me – about greetings".

You decide when to continue walking

Repeat your training at different speeds. Run – stop suddenly, walk quickly – stop suddenly, walk slowly – sudden stop, run – walk. Obedience training is based on teaching the dog to follow your pace. Make sure that it is you, not the dog, who reinitiates motion after a stop. Count to three before starting the walk!

Change of pace with distractions

As the dog becomes obedient in distraction-free situations, it is time to take his training to the next level by introducing distraction or rewards right in front of him. Place or throw something your dog wants about 30-50 yards in front of you. The distance is important. You will be stopping a few times on the way. The closer the distraction, the more difficult it is to keep your dog's attention!

Start with pace change that is most familiar for the dog: run – sudden stop. Your dog will get his reward if he stops when you do, and before the leash is tight. Then you should tell the dog "go ahead" and let go of the leash. Make sure your dog doesn't reach his target when he lunges, but is allowed to run only as a reward for heeding your change of pace! If the dog makes a mistake by pulling on the leash, repeat the same thing again: run – sharp stop. Only reward the dog for stopping before hitting the end of the leash.

Remember to vary your rewards. Sometimes reward your dog with play or treats, sometimes say "go ahead" and offer freedom.

Isaac – not a very obedient fellow

I met Lisa and Isaac, her four-year-old Doberman, on a course. She complained that Isaac couldn't walk properly with a leash. We took a walk so that I could see what the real problem was. The behavioral pattern soon became clear. Every time Isaac pulled on the leash, Lisa stopped. Isaac then came immediately back to her and stood at her left side. As soon as Lisa started walking again, Isaac took off and stretched the leash to its full length. Lisa stopped again and Isaac ran back, and this was repeated again and again. The error was that Lisa focused on what she should do when Isaac started to pull, instead of teaching him to match her tempo. In that way she became a disciplinarian instead of a facilitator. Lisa had to go into training tempo changes and teach Isaac that he had to stop and make contact when she stopped – before the leash was stretched out. She also had to teach him positive leash jerks.

HIDE & SEEK ON LEASH

Another way of teaching a dog on-leash willingness to follow is to use the "Hide and Seek" exercise described in the chapter "Who follows whom? About contact training and obedience training". Behave as you do when you train the dog off leash – run away! Let go of the leash and take off in a different direction. In the beginning, hold your training sessions in quiet environments. Before long, you can let go of the leash even if you find yourself in other situations.

Build on the Hide and Seek exercise and train in different environments. Try dropping the leash, and then stop. How long does it take your dog to discover you are no longer attached to the leash? What happens if you let go of the leash and continue walking in the same direction as your dog, before you run away? This exercise is based on creating uncertainty. Suddenly, you're not there! Your dog will consequently keep better tabs on you, becoming more obedient in the process.

Give the leash to a friend

You can also have someone else help. While you stand there chatting with friend, let go of the leash or hand it him or her. Don't let your dog see what just happened. Then walk away. Look over your shoulder, but don't engage or praise your dog until he tries to make eye contact with you and takes a few steps towards you.

Use this same exercise when you go for a walk with another dog owner. Wait until the dog has settled down, then try dropping the leash and sneaking away. There is no need always to go in a different direction. What happens if you run forwards? Does your dog follow you? If you are not confident enough, you can always quietly hand the leash to your friend and then sneak away. How long time does it take before your dog notices you are gone? Also, sneak away with your dog's favorite toy in plain sight. This adds an extra incentive!

LEASH JERKS – THE ULTIMATE NO-NO?

In the eyes of some dog owners, deliberately jerking on the leash is akin to a mortal sin. Others claim that it is simply impossible to teach a dog to walk calmly on a leash without correcting him when he pulls.

Leash jerks: contact, not correction

Sometimes I ask my students what their dog does when he feels a jerk on his neck and how they would like their dogs to react. For example, what happens if I teach the dog that a light tug on the leash might result in a reward if he initiates contact with me? A light jerk essentially creates contact instead of a correction. I use small peppy jerks now and then on my dogs when we are out for a walk. I tug, and as soon as they look at me, I reward them for making contact. Then we continue on the walk.

Begin the training in a neutral situation, when your dog is beside or ahead of you. It helps to show you have treats before starting. Begin with light, playful tugs on the leash. This is preferable to a hard jerk. By using light jerks, you desensitize the dog's neck. As soon as your dog looks at you, speak to him, then back up and give a treat on either side. You can also turn and walk in the other direction. Be sure to praise the dog as soon as he appears at your side.

Small jerks signal a change of pace

A jerk on the leash can signal a change of pace. This can have faster results than if you just stop and wait for the dog to stop on his own. Make a dead stop at the same time as you jerk the leash. After a few times, you should only have to stop for the dog to realize that he also has to stop. This is another way of communicating with your dog, independent of the leash. The dog will react to your change of pace rather than seeking contact only when the leash tightens.

LEAD THE DOG WITH YOUR BODY – TAKE YOUR SEATS!

When the dog finds an interesting scent, your most natural reaction is often to try pulling him away from the scent patch. But think! You are probably standing behind the dog trying to make him follow you. Can the dog see you? What about claiming the scent patch for yourself? What happens if you calmly and firmly stand on the scent patch, effectively saying "This is mine!"

Teach the dog to back up

One training method is to teach the dog to move away whenever you move towards him. This has several advantages. The larger the dog, the more important it is you can control him using your body.

Start the lesson by focusing on a scent that has caught your dog's interest. Keep the leash short, so you can control the dog if he tries to get past you. Move slowly, silently and forcefully towards the dog, either from the front or the side. Avoid sudden movements that might cause stress. Rest a little on your heels with each step. The dog will most likely stand still at first, wondering what you are doing. Keep the pressure on, even if it means you have to bump into the dog. Immediately praise the dog when he starts moving away and makes eye contact with you. Tell him "go ahead" and allow him to investigate the odor. This now gives you a new reward for your toolbox. Then you can vary the kinds of rewards – with a treat or by continuing your walk together.

Reading suggestion: Read more about internal and external rewards in the chapter "Become a better teacher – about learning theory".

The dog must win by cooperating – everyday heeling

You probably don't want your dog to lunge upon meeting a fellow canine. Therefore, avoid allowing your dog to pull from side to side even in other situations. Meeting other dogs will become considerably less eventful if your dog knows never to cross your path.

Teach your dog to walk on your right hand side when you hold the leash in your right hand and vice versa – leash in the left hand means the dog should remain on the left. Walk so you are closest to the good smells at the side of the road, so your dog doesn't always have free access to them. Shorten the leash by half to keep your dog from crossing in front of you. When he starts walking calmly and stops pulling, reward him directly by moving the leash to your other hand and saying "go ahead". This cue means that your dog can sniff to his heart's content. After a while, resume the training.

Gradually make the training more difficult by increasing how long your dog must walk obediently before you release him with "go ahead", and grant permission to switch sides.

Training tips: use a head halter

Is walking on a leash an ordeal for both you and your dog? Then you should exchange the collar for a head halter. This works in the same way as a halter on a horse: when the dog pulls forward, his head will automatically turn backwards towards your hand. This means he no longer has the physical power to pull. The disadvantage is that the head halter looks like a muzzle, which some people might disagree with. A simple solution is to sew a brightly colored ribbon onto the halter to raise curiosity, rather than suspicion. Using the head halter is seldom a solution to the problem; however, it is a tool to help you succeed with your training. You cannot teach your dog if you are constantly aggravated or afraid of not being able to hold him. Be sure that you never jerk on the head halter, particularly not when the leash is loose. There is always a risk of injury if the dog's neck is exposed to hard jerks.

WHY DOES MY DOG BITE THE LEASH?

Puppies naturally bite the leash because the leash simply invites play. However, it may also become an effective command to the owner to walk in a different direction. At the start of a walk, dogs might have excess energy to burn. At this time, even the adult dog may pull or bite the leash. Maybe you only engage the dog during the walk when he does something wrong? In that case, negative attention is better than no attention. In addition, some dogs feel more secure when they are holding something in their mouth. Just like babies and pacifiers!

Sometimes the dog will chew on the leash out of frustration or when he is at a loss about what to do, perhaps when you just stand there listening to your instructor. Some dogs will chew on the leash when they pass other dogs. Dogs that do not understand what is happening, maybe because they have become mentally tired, will also often react by biting the leash.

Aggravation can increase biting behaviors

Depending on our reaction to chewing, we might reinforce a behavior that can become a serious bone of contention. The situation can become much worse if we get upset or angry because the dog does not listen. The louder your voice becomes and the more you jerk and pull on the leash, the greater the chance your dog will block you out entirely.

Instead of calming down, he will bite the leash even more. You might provoke your dog rather than disrupt an undesirable behavior.

Reward your dog's spontaneous interaction

You might try temporarily switching to a leash with a chain at the base, which is not nearly as tempting to chew. Then focus on rewarding your dog's spontaneous interactions with you. Bring some extra special goodies that your dog will get only when he walks calmly. Reward your dog with various activities. If the biting is a relatively new behavior, it may be enough to stop, avert your eyes and wait for the dog to calm down. You can also casually drop the leash and continue to walk. The earlier you observe this behavior, the less the chance that he starts chewing. Above all, work to prevent unwanted behaviors. Which behavior will you pay attention to? Do you want your dog to be quiet and calm when you stand still? If so, then offer a reward.

Water – cleans more than hands

It is hard to correct a behavior that is based on attention seeking. If ignoring the dog does not work, a correction might work. Use a small water-filled bottle that you keep hidden in your hand. An empty soap bottle will work fine. The point of this method is to surprise the dog without him realizing that the correction comes from you. Learn to recognize the dog's mood before he starts biting the leash. As soon as your dog begins to grab at the leash, swiftly pour the water on his head. At the same time, keep sauntering forwards with the attitude: "What just happened?" Let the dog absorb what has occurred before you pay attention to him again, and then only when he walks obediently by your side.

WHY DOES MY DOG REFUSE TO WALK ON THE LEASH?

Early one morning when I was out for a walk, I spotted a dog owner with her cute longhaired dachshund. The dog stopped frequently and right then the woman's hand went into her pocket fishing for a treat. The dog trotted happily up to his owner's side, swallowed the treat and followed along for a couple of yards. Then he slammed on the brakes and got another treat. I smiled and asked myself if I ought to walk up and tell the woman why her dog kept stopping. Wise from experience, I refrained. People seldom appreciate unsolicited advice. I just quietly observed that this woman had fallen into the correction trap – she was rewarding the wrong behavior.

Preventative leash training involves focusing on correct behavior. Give high value rewards when the dog does what you want him to, and not for anything related to making mistakes, such as refusing to walk. If your dog slams on his brakes, quietly continue walking without looking at him. You can also try dropping the leash and continue walking if you are in a safe environment. Make sure you reward the dog only when he walks beside you or near you. In this way, you reorient the dog's thinking: Mom isn't any fun if he stops, only when he walks beside her.

Training tip: take a break

One problem with teaching a dog to walk properly on a leash is that it's impossible to be consistent throughout the entire walk. Both of us need a break from training. Teach a release cue, so that both you and your dog can relax for a minute. If you are tired of training, you can put the leash under one of the dog's front legs. This will impede his ability to pull. Even if your dog starts pulling, he won't have the same power. This isn't a very effective method with short-legged breeds, as they will just lift their front paw and the brake is gone. You will have to find another cue for taking a break from training. A halter or harness might do the trick.

UNLEASH THE DOG: CONTACT SIGNALS FREEDOM

Most dog owners have some kind of ritual associated with taking the leash off and letting the dog run free. For example, this may involve having the dog sit and waiting for him to make eye contact before he gets his cue for "free". If you vary the situation, it will increase the dog's attention and obedience. No matter when, where and how you unleash the dog, and regardless if you sit, stand, walk or run, the dog must not be allowed to leave you until you give him the signal, such as "go ahead". Vary the time when you give the cue. Don't teach your dog he is allowed to run free or start working the minute the leash comes off. Increase the waiting time from the moment you take the leash off until you give the cue by a couple of seconds at a time. Be consistent in expecting your dog to stay calm and attentive. Hold the initial training sessions in quiet surroundings with no distractions from people and animals.

Once the dog has understood he must make eye contact with you to get his cue for "free", start testing him by turning your back on him or moving away at the same time as you are calling him. When he comes to your left side and makes contact, immediately give him the coveted cue for "free". Rewarding contact with a cue for "free" in a variety of situations will increase your dog's attention and obedience! If you stay consistent with your cue as your dog is by your left side, you will get a positive side effect: you teach your dog to walk close to you, without a leash.

SUMMARY:

- Walking calmly on the leash is the same as being obedient!
- Train your dog to walk calmly on a leash by changing pace and direction. Reward when the dog when he initiates contact!
- Don't let the dog to reach his goal when he lunges on the leash!
- Activate the dog when he is on the leash!
- You cannot possibly train during the whole walk – use a cue for "free" to take a break.

Help! My dog growls!

Contents:

When a dog growls, he is usually saying he wants some space. However, sometimes growling means your dog is in high spirits. This is known as "talking". For example, retrievers often talk when they greet you, and Rottweilers have been known to "rumble".

Many people become alarmed when a dog growls, and feel threatened by the low-pitched sound. In order to interpret the type of growl we are dealing with, we have to observe the dog's other signals. Dogs that growl as a threat are on guard with tense muscles. On the other hand, if a dog is talking, he is relaxed. He might wag his tail or let you know he wants to be petted. He might also carry something around in his mouth.

GROWLING INDICATES DISTRUST

In most cases, the threatening growl is about lack of trust between dog and human. By growling, the dog wants to be left alone. A dog school outside of Stockholm also had a program for re-homing dogs. One of their residents was a lively, charming golden retriever named Kasper. After trying to bite the kids in his original family, he was a candidate for re-homing due to his aggression. After two failed re-homings, I decided to adopt him.

Kasper, a wise instructor on the subject of aggression

The first time Kasper tried to bite me was when we had a battle on the rug in my study. I was convinced that I should discipline him in such a way he would never again dare to be aggressive. This was of course to the opposite approach to what my teacher had taught me about handling aggressive dogs. But I was young, immature and ignorant and convinced I knew what I was doing.

Kasper's aggression surfaced in the presence of children, as well as near his food bowl, and in tight spaces. If I moved around in the kitchen during Kasper's dinner, he would stop eating, lift his head and bare his teeth. The slightest attention would unleash a display of extreme aggression. One of my colleagues once made the mistake of trying to touch him when he was eating, and he bit her pretty badly on her arm. It was only after I fed him by hand for a few weeks that he let me take his food bowl. Later on, anyone could walk by him when he was eating without triggering his defense mechanisms.

Could Kasper ever be trusted not to bite? No, we couldn't leave him tied up anywhere as someone might come up and pet him or a child might try to hug him.

Why did I even bother adopting such an aggressive dog? Why didn't I put him to sleep the first time he bit? I kept Kasper because most of the time he was a happy, charming dog who loved to work. I was convinced I would be able to train him and make his dark side disappear.

It turned out we were very successful in competition, and Kasper even became an obedience champion. This showed just how complex the human-canine relationship really is. Not every problem can be solved with dominance. His behavior is determined by a combination of past and current experience. I discovered that Kasper was at his most aggressive when he felt threatened. Then he didn't even trust me. If I had responded to him with aggression in this situation, I would have never been able to gain his trust.

It turned out several of Kasper's littermates also had low aggression thresholds. Given a different start in life and more knowledgeable owners, this predisposition might never have developed. However, Kasper's original family had never had a dog before. Taking on an adult dog with aggression problems is a huge responsibility, not only for the people involved, but also for the dog. One must remember that this is about a wounded soul and that such a dog might never become completely rehabilitated.

Kasper and I made everyday life work, because I didn't have kids and neither did those in my social circle. My task was to shelter him from activities that made him aggressive. I don't think I would ever have had such insight into aggression if Kasper had not been in my life for five years.

THE GROWL – A SIGN OF INSECURITY?

A growl is a signal that many people interpret as an insult or as assertive. This reasoning is hierarchical: a younger or lower-ranked individual has no right to assert himself. However, it is not at all clear that dogs growl because we are not sufficiently dominant. In my experience, growling most often indicates lack of trust and the dog's desire to get some distance from the receiver. I highly doubt that dogs growl to assert their rank.

Growling often occurs in specific situations. Dogs may be distrustful in a specific situation. In other situations, the relationship may function completely fine. Therefore, it's important to analyze what triggers the behavior. On the other hand, if we continue rehashing the problem, it can affect our overall relationship with the dog in question. Much too often we try to address a situation by responding with aggression. However, is there another, more effective approach?

Mick growls at Mom

Mick, a Briard, only growled at his mom Anna when he was lying down in his bed. She had been advised to grab him and "make him mind" when this happened. Instead, he growled even more. Consequently, Anna's own aggression towards Mick increased. When they came to see me, their relationship was so toxic that Mick would attack Anna if she walked by him in the dark.

I asked Anna to ignore all growls and not respond with anger. She was to avert her gaze and yawn when she went past Mick to indicate friendliness. In addition, she was to drop some treats regardless of whether he growled.

Anna worried that this might reward his behavior. But the dog's negative reactions changed when Anna started throwing treats to him. Instead, he started looking expectantly at Anna when she walked by. After a couple of days, Mick stopped growling. Anna then started giving him the treats less frequently, and sometimes only after petting him. It turned out that Mick's growls only meant he wanted to be left alone. By ignoring him and offering him something he wanted, Anna neutralized the situation.

WHEN THE DOG GROWLS AT BEING HANDLED

A dog growls at people for many different reasons. The dog may be sick, or he might have not had enough social training as a puppy. If the dog suddenly starts to growl at one particular person in the family, we usually interpret this as a relationship problem. Find out why the dog wants to increase the distance to the person in question. If the growling is due illness, it is not unusual that the dog will direct his growling towards the person who activates and plays with him the most. The dog does not have the strength to play and growls to discourage the activity.

Incorrect handling can cause aggression

Misinterpreting or incorrectly handling a young dog, for instance while cutting his nails, might lead to aggressive behavior as an adult to avoid the same situation. The dog's aggression is not so much due to nail cutting, but rather being restrained. I see it as a lack of trust between dog and owner.

Examining the dog may also cause him to growl. The dog growls to try to increase the distance and get away from being close. The growl is not an attempt to dominate, as is often believed.

Kasper, whom I told you about before, probably never had an unpleasant experience with nail cutting or teeth cleaning. He would sit quietly at the veterinarian's with a jaw block in his mouth and allow anyone to look down his throat. He had confidence in me and trusted the situations in which I put him.

Bimbo bites during ear and eye care

An older couple consulted me when their terrier Bimbo bit them when they tried to clean his eyes and ears. Correcting Bimbo was not an option. He knew he could bite to avoid the treatment, so corrections increased rather than decreased his aggression.

We chose to create an activity exercise in connection with general care. First, we taught Bimbo that the sound of a clicker meant a treat. Then we put a towel on the floor with treats on top. When he went to the towel and started eating, we clicked once for each time he stretched for a new treat. When Bimbo left the towel, we took it away and waited five minutes. Then we repeated the same exercise. The third time we brought out the towel we did not put any treats on it. Bimbo went there anyhow, thanks to his previous positive experiences. When he stepped on the towel, we rewarded this behavior by clicking and throwing a treat on it. After a number of repetitions, Bimbo ran happily and willingly to the towel.

Then we took the training to the next level and put some cotton swabs and medicine on the towel. After some hesitation, he went there and stood on it. We talked normally and did not show any interest in Bimbo at all, but I kept an eye on him so I could reward him at the right time.

When Bimbo was able to walk up to and stand on the towel with no problem, we started touching and grabbing him before we clicked for the correct behavior. There were times when we moved too fast and he ran away, which we allowed. When Bimbo became aware that he could run away if he felt threatened, and that nobody forced him to stay, he started coming back more quickly. It seemed like he gradually braced himself to continue standing there until he heard the click. His self-confidence grew and he enjoyed the training.

Every time we introduced something new, like picking up the cotton swab from the towel or bringing out the tube of eye ointment, we clicked to reward him for staying. If the clicks were too late, he reacted by running away. This told us we had missed some important step in the training. We analyzed what triggered his reaction and on the next occasion, we were rewarded the correct behavior more quickly. His desire to run away decreased little by little and gradually it ceased altogether.

Step by step, we trained Bimbo to allow us to look in his ears, then to caress the inside of his ear with a cotton ball, and lastly to let us to wipe his ears. I felt that Bimbo liked the challenge if he was allowed to remain standing until I clicked for the right behavior. This training took a couple of weeks, but during this time, the trust between Bimbo and his owners improved considerably.

Passive cooperation leads to freedom

It is seldom possible to get a growling dog to accept care and treatment with domination. However, if we change our behavior from restraining the dog to cooperating with him, then his reasons for biting also disappear. Teaching a puppy from the beginning to remain quiet to get freedom is the foundation for a large part of our dog training. The dog will accept treatment because he knows his passive cooperation will lead to freedom. The training I did with Max in the example below is easy with rapid results.

Reading suggestion: Read more about passivity training in the chapter: "On/off! About environmental training and passivity training".

Max does not want to have his paws wiped

Max was a terrier that bit his owner whenever his paws were wiped. A veterinary exam showed the dog had problems with his back and pasterns and we put him on anti-inflammatory medications. However, the problem remained. Max was expecting pain whenever anyone twisted his paws or stretched his rear legs in a certain way. By growling or showing his teeth, Max tried to tell his owner to stop wiping his paws. I sat down on a chair and let Max realize I had a bowl of treats with me. When he approached, I taught him the world's most common trick. I had a treat in my hand and just waited for him to raise a paw from the floor the slightest bit. That is when I gave him a treat. After a couple of repetitions, Max had learned to put his paw in my open hand before he got the treat. I repeated every training sequence three times before we took a half-minute break allowing the dog time to better absorb the lessons from the training. Meanwhile, I ignored Max. The next time I waved the treat, Max immediately approached and lifted his paw up to my hand. I gradually increased the degree of difficulty to the point where

I could close my hand around his paw. Sometimes he would pull it back, but he never growled, because I gave him the possibility of interrupting the activity himself. I never said anything to him but just calmly waited for him. He always returned and lifted his paw up to my hand to get his reward.

His realization that there would be no reward when he pulled his paw away led to silent cooperation. Max had to figure out how to get me to give him the reward. I grabbed and petted his paw, he winced but kept his paw still and I rewarded him. When I advanced the training to the point of taking out a towel, Max became more suspicious, although he stayed put. He reluctantly lifted his paw and got his reward. If he put his paw down, I ignored it and waited quietly until he put his paw back in my hand by himself.

Reading suggestion: In the chapter "When the problem is a fact – turning conflict into control," you can read more about conflicts surrounding cleaning, general care and treatments.

WHEN THE DOG GUARDS OBJECTS

Many dogs keep careful watch over their own and others' possessions. If they feel their treasures are threatened, they will respond in kind. It is seldom possible to solve this type of problem by competing with the dog for control of the object. Instead, we need to teach the dog to fetch and bring the treasure to us. This is a good basis for cooperation rather than competition.

Teach the dog to fetch and bring his treasure to you

A good method for eliminating these kinds of problems is to teach the dog to fetch and bring his treasure to you. Start by introducing your dog to the sound of the clicker. The dog has to learn that the sound of the clicker means that a reward, such as a treat, is on its way. Put out an object that holds no interest for you. Sit down calmly and pretend not to be interested in what the dog is doing. You could pretend to read a newspaper or watch TV.

The instant the dog seizes the object, reward him by clicking and throw some treats his way. When the immediate surprise subsides, he will probably seize the object again. Reward this behavior again by clicking and throwing treats down about two feet away from him.

When the dog drops the object and moves away to eat the treats, this creates distance to the object. Gradually increase the distance between the place where the dog grasps the object and the place where you throw the treats. Be careful not to throw the treats close to you, until the dog starts looking at you when he has the object in his mouth. Otherwise you risk turning the situation into something competitive. You don't want the dog to think you are eager to get the object.

If the dog drops the object before you have clicked, pretend like nothing happened and just devote yourself to your newspaper. Wait for the dog to grab the object again and look at you. Then click and throw the treat – in any direction but yours.

Advanced training in different situations

For advanced training, use a variety of objects and do the training in those situations where there usually is a problem. Be sure to use objects the dog views as desirable. This puts you in control. The simplest way is to drop the object behind you when you go for a walk and then do the exercise on the way back.

Continue to train the dog every day. Then start gradually throwing the treats in between you and the dog. Put them down closer and closer to where you are standing. Finally, they end up in your hand. At that point, take the object from the dog's mouth before you click and give him a treat. You can also work without the clicker. Don't speak, as your voice, no matter what tone you use, will likely communicate competition to your dog. Instead, remain silent with a neutral demeanor. Don't say "give" and throw down the treats until your dog looks at you with the object in his mouth and expectation in his eyes. Repeat the exercise five to ten times. Then try saying "give" without throwing treats. If your dog drops the object? Time for a treat!

Make sure you don't always grab the object immediately. Otherwise, the dog might start perceiving the object as something very valuable. Throw the treats away from the dog, so you can calmly walk up and take the object – your dog is busy searching for treats. This method is based on trust-building. Your goal should be to teach your dog to fetch and bring the objects he finds – not to stop taking things in his mouth.

Alfons – the county sanitation worker

Maria and her soft coated Wheaten terrier Alfons had differing opinions about what to do with "found" objects. Alfons picked up pieces of paper, chewing gum and anything else he deemed valuable. Maria kept trying to take objects out of his mouth when they went for a walk. After awhile, Alfons ended up guarding all kinds of objects - a situation that was stressful, worrisome and not much fun.

To get rid of the problem, Maria had to learn to reward Alfons every time he picked up something he found. When I met them again a couple of months later, she told me that Alfons was now the new county sanitation worker. Not only did he pick up trash from others, he went to the nearest trash can, jumped up with his front paws and dropped trash in. Then he got his reward. Talk about mixing business with pleasure!

Don't compete

If any correction at all is warranted when the dog guards an object, it has to happen before the dog seizes the object. This doesn't leave any time for any kind of competition to develop between you and your dog. The type of correction you use is also decisive. A social correction, like physically grabbing the dog, unfortunately often triggers aggression. The dog might also try to swallow his treasure before you get to him or run away to eat it.

If you do use correction, use the element of surprise. If your dog turns around after being corrected, he should see you pretending to be busy with something else. A useful surprise correction is to spray water on the dog using a spray bottle. You can also throw something at or close to the dog without him seeing where it comes from. If your dog tries to initiate contact with you after you correct him, you should be friendly and receptive. Redirect him, so he doesn't see you picking up the object. This is particularly important in the beginning, when competition is at the forefront of your dog's mind. As soon as your training is successful, the sense of competition will disappear.

Reading suggestion: Read more about corrections in the chapter "Correction – or revenge?"

WHEN THE DOG GUARDS HIS BOWL

Ethologically speaking, everyone in a pack has a right to defend his/her food. This makes it difficult to use corrections to stop this type of activity. Guarding his food bowl is not a way for the dog to ascend in some hierarchy, but rather defending food he thinks is about to be stolen. Don't start competing over the food – the risk of aggression is too great. This type of guarding behavior will become worse if the dog cannot understand why his food has been taken. He will view it as competition for prey.

Become a teammate – not a competitor

If the competition has been going on for some time and you're afraid that the dog will bite, it is better to start putting one piece of food in the bowl at a time. He will gradually get used to the idea that you are not a competitor, but rather an asset. The dog will see that you provide food, rather than steal it. At the same time, sit down quietly and watch TV or read a newspaper. It is important that you are completely disinterested and don't allow yourself to be provoked, to ensure the dog feels you are not competing for the same food.

Meanwhile, you can also try eating something the dog would prefer to his own food. When he has finished eating and is about to leave his bowl, call him and drop a piece of your delicious food into his bowl. As soon as this works, walk up to the bowl just as he is finishing and drop the goody. Continue the training by approaching the food bowl earlier and earlier, while the dog is still eating, and drop your treat into the bowl. Never look at the dog or speak to him either as you approach him. The only signals you should be using are those that prevent his aggression, like yawning and averting your gaze, which demonstrates you are not competing over the food.

SUMMARY

- Growls often mean the dog doesn't trust you
- Dogs growl to increase distance from others.
- The fact that the dog growls in particular situations does not always mean you have a bad relationship in general.
- Responding to a growling dog with dominance can increase his aggression.
- Don't compete with a dog that guards objects. Instead, teach him to fetch!

Bregott

Correction – or revenge

Contents:

No topic is as controversial as that of corrections. There are certain dog owners and trainers who categorically deny the need for corrections. Others see corrections as way to raise children or dogs – to establish respect. We know that children who are exposed to constant nagging and inappropriate corrections act out and have difficulty trusting. In addition, they will be quick to defend themselves. There are no reasons to expect dogs to react any differently.

Can you correct a dog without creating insecurity and frustration? In my experience, when corrections are given in anger, they might trigger fear, flight or defense mechanisms. In order for a correction to have any kind of a positive effect, we must block out all frustration and aggression. Those kinds of emotions will diminish the dog's trust of our relationship: he does not feel secure when we are together. We can control our emotions by planning ahead – corrections must be deliberate, just like any other type of training.

CORRECTIONS MUST INTERRUPT WHEN THE DOG MAKES A MISTAKE

A correction is an action that makes the dog stop an unwanted behavior. It gives you breathing room – not a permanent change. Do not assume the dog will do the right thing the next time just because you corrected him when he did something wrong. What do you want the dog to do instead? That's the behavior you really need to teach him.

Correcting presumes willingness

A correction usually means something unpleasant. It may involve telling the dog "No!", clearing your throat, stepping on the leash, or spraying water on him. If a correction is to be effective, there must be a mutual willingness to cooperate, otherwise there is no point. If the dog doesn't want to be together with you, then he has nothing to lose. In that case, the correction will have no effect.

A correction might also involve withholding an expected reward, in the same way as children who have misbehaved forgo candy or their allowance. However, this presupposes the dog will actively work to receive rewards. Otherwise, the dog will not perceive these actions as corrections.

Reading suggestion: Read more about rewards in the chapter "Become a better teacher – about learning theory".

Prevention or correction?

We frequently use corrections because we have not taught the dog the behavior we actually want. The more you focus on prevention by teaching basic obedience, the fewer incorrect behaviors your dog will display, and the fewer corrections you will need to make. It is up to you to decide whether you want to emphasize prevention or correction. People who work more with correction-based training focus primarily on mistakes. The dog does something wrong, and is corrected. He is praised when he stops the behavior in question. This might be true, but a dog owner who wholeheartedly believes corrections will make for an obedient and happy dog may want to think again. A "no" followed by "good" can turn into a trap where everything is focused on finding faults. It is impossible to develop a strong relationship on the basis of prohibitions, supervision and nagging. Eventually, this type of relationship will lead to mistrust, regardless of whether we are dealing with people or dogs. In the long run, the relationship will founder.

A dam corrects her pups in many different ways

Quite frequently, we find our corrections compared to the behavior of the dam and her puppies. Many say that a dam will push the puppy to the ground by grabbing onto the skin of his neck. "In actuality, the dam will turn the puppy over to groom and clean him, not in order to correct him. When it comes to the dam's care of her puppies, I have seldom heard anybody explain this behavior in terms of anything other than dominance. How do we know that dominance is the most important part in the relation between a dam and her pup? Why not her care and grooming? Many dog moms spend a lot more time playing with their pups than correcting them. Why is it difficult to believe we can create a good relationship with our dog without using aggression?

Indifference – also a correction

It is hard to draw general conclusions from a specific correction a dam may use with her puppy. There is logic to how the dog acts towards her puppy in a specific situation. On another occasion, she may ignore her puppy rather than use a physical correction. Older dogs tend to have infinite patience with the younger ones in a pack. They seldom use aggression if they can instead walk away or display disinterest. The social life in a pack is not about extremes. Dogs use many kinds of signals to communicate. These signals are often too rapid and minute for us to pick up on. We see behavior that we misinterpret as aggression. However, how many of us understand why older dogs ignore the younger ones, and recognize its value?

"He's a Rottweiler!"

A young couple with their first dog, a Rottweiler, attended one of my puppy classes. The larger the puppy became, the more they wanted to use domination when he did something wrong. I tried in vain to help them change their attitude about how to foster a good relationship with their puppy. "He is a Rottweiler!" They came to class less and less frequently. Their desire to control the dog through dominance was greater than their desire to build a relationship through cooperation. It was easy to throw the young dog on his back when he was a pup. However, as he grew physically and mentally, he started objecting to such treatment. The woman had more and more difficulty expressing herself in terms of dominance, as soon as the dog discovered he could overpower her. In the end, the dog was re-homed. The attitude of this couple - who believed that dominance and aggression were the way to demand respect from their pet – only taught the pup to defend himself when he felt threatened. I hope that the dog ended up with a new owner who taught him there is no need for fighting within in a pack.

Tough or numb?

Dogs can "shut down" and become unresponsive when we lean over them, hiss at them or threaten them to make them listen. Nagging and frustration have nothing to do with correcting. Screaming, pleading and nagging to get respect are as ineffective among dogs as among people. A dog that is frequently punished will protect himself against discomfort and pain. He will just learn to endure more. When the dog cannot avoid corrections, he tends to shut down both physically and emotionally – he becomes numb. As time goes by, it becomes more and more difficult to communicate with him. Using more and more severe forms of punishment creates a vicious cycle of corrections, where the dog shuts down more and more. At that point, we start perceiving the dog as tough and stubborn.

Think about:

Do you correct your dog to stop the wrong behavior or to show him "who is the boss"? Do you correct your dog because someone close to you expects it?

CORRECT WITHOUT VALUE JUDGMENT – DIFFICULT BUT NECESSARY

When the dog makes a mistake, we often become victims of our own emotions. We become frustrated and we feel powerless when our dog does not respect our commands. Using corrections, we can express these emotions. In addition, sometimes our behavior will be guided by other people's reactions. The dog's action made us lose face in front of others. The dog, our best friend, let us down. We are forced to stand there, "caught with our pants down", and expose ourselves to the reactions of others. It is easy to understand why frustration and anger play such a disproportionately large role when it comes to bringing up our four-legged friends.

Correction – or revenge?

Many people regard correction and aggression as the same thing – and that we must feel angry in order to correct. I don't think so! Corrections, when you lose your cool, are seldom effective. You are emotionally blocked and are unable to read your dog's communicative signals at that moment, nor do you have any desire to do so. The most common mistake is to act threateningly or aggressively despite the dog having stopped his misbehavior. Perhaps he stopped and turned towards you, but you still confront him in anger. The dog is doing the right thing, but is nevertheless corrected anyhow – due to your temper. This is when the correction is no longer a correction, just a sign of bad judgment. A good trainer once told a dog owner, when the latter threw his dog to the ground in a fit of anger and frustration, "What you are doing right now is not correction – it is revenge!"

Think about:

Do you often become extremely angry when your dog does something wrong? Don't put your head in the sand – realize you have a problem. What is the state of your relationship with your dog? Is it based on nagging and misplaced corrections? Do you enjoy each other when you are together? Do you think that the results will be better when the dog knows that you are the one doing the corrections?

THE UNINTENDED CONSEQUENCES OF CORRECTIONS

Before we correct the dog, we must ask: how do we want the dog to perceive the correction? Don't assume that corrections will necessarily stop a behavior. Problems with recalls often depend on us having used improper corrections. When we call the dog and he doesn't respond, we then try to coerce the dog into obeying by using an angry voice. However, if the dog is unresponsive, our anger will not be effective. The dog is still interested in investigating his immediate environment. He may have also learned to stay out of the way when we are angry. Instead, our aggression makes it difficult for the dog to come close. Who would voluntarily approach someone who is angry? The solution is not to use more corrections and become even angrier. It takes skill and planning for the correction not to become a pattern that is repeated over and over again. Repeated corrections in specific situations are trouble, and will ultimately damage the relationship.

The wrong correction may become a reward

The wrong corrections may have completely different consequences than the ones you intend. We often correct a dog for barking at strange sounds. As soon as the dog becomes quiet, we praise him. However, why did the dog become quiet? Was it due to your correction, or was he silent so he could hear better? If you praise the dog for being quiet while he is still focused on the sound, then you might be rewarding the behavior that you intended to correct. In other words, you have to be very careful for a correction really to have the intended consequence.

DIFFERENT DOGS – DIFFERENT CORRECTIONS

Not all dogs should be corrected in the same way. A correction that makes one dog immediately stop his behavior might make another dog go into defense mode. Others might back away and refuse to initiate contact with you for several hours. It might also depend on breed. For example, a Labrador, when subjected to physical corrections, is less likely to display aggression towards his owner than a terrier, a breed that can become extremely hostile. Thus, knowledge about breeds and individual dogs is essential when using corrections. Another example is that quite a few owners of Dachshunds can testify to the fact that a sharp command will send a wiener dog for a lengthy pouting session in his basket. The way our dogs – and we – react to corrections is based on personality and previous experience.

Tarraz – not just any old dog

I got started working as a dog psychologist in the 1980s and at this time "ethologically correct corrections" were typical. In other words, I threw dogs on their backs when I thought it was justified. During my education at a school in Stockholm, I was one of those working with a German shepherd named Tarraz. He was an unfriendly creature, and most people went out of their way to avoid him. Over time, I developed a good relationship with Tarraz, and we planned to place him as a security dog.

Ben, a professional trainer, appeared one morning with a security guard named Henry. We went for a walk so Henry would get to know Tarraz. Along the way, we passed an exercise yard. Tarraz was actually quite friendly towards other dogs, but this morning he made a couple of forceful lunges towards one of the dogs in the exercise yard. My correction technique was well established, and some seconds later Tarraz was on his back. After a while, he calmed down and relaxed, so I let him up, pet him, and we continued on our walk.

Then Henry took over handling Tarraz, who immediately started pulling on the leash. Henry tried to correct Tarraz, but the dog completely ignored him. I unsuccessfully tried to convince Henry to change his tactics and explained he should become friends with the dog first. I was a 23-year-old rookie and he was an older, experienced dog handler.

This did not go down well. We were walking along a back yard guarded by a barking chow. Tarraz lunged, and Henry corrected him for the umpteenth time with the leash. Tarraz responded promptly and bit Henry on the shoulder and arm. During the rest of the walk, Henry did not put any demands at all on Tarraz, whom he had totally misjudged. Because I used corrections, I had probably authorized tougher methods – methods that not just anyone could use on Tarraz. I could correct Tarraz because he trusted me. In hindsight, I believe I used an unnecessary amount of force.

Henry made the mistake of starting the relationship by trying to demand respect – with the wrong type of dog. Not all dogs can be corrected physically and not by just anybody. Their response is anger. If you accept this challenge, you had better be so convincing that the dog never dares to repeat his behavior. Bearing that in mind, the risk is huge that in the next situation the dog will respond both with more speed and aggression. What did he learn then?

PLAN YOUR CORRECTIONS

If you are going to teach the dog to discontinue a bad behavior, you must proceed in exactly the same way as you would with any other training. You need a plan. What triggers the dog's behavior? Do you need any equipment? Where will you do it? How far away from the dog will you be? Do not put any value judgments in the correction – just consider what behavior you are going to correct, when you will do it, and how you will do it.

Planning gives you control

By preparing for the correction as you would any other obedience exercise, you will be one step ahead. Planning ahead gives you control both over your own emotions and of the situation. My Swedish editor, Eliza Kajanus, said during a discussion about corrections, "With planning, we will almost be happy when the dog does something wrong, because then we can stop the behavior. On the other hand, if the dog makes a mistake *without* planning we tend to be furious."

Reading suggestion: Read about how learning works and how to plan the lesson in the chapter "Become a better teacher – about learning theory".

Stage a crime spree

For successful corrections, you must put your dog in a situation that will trigger the undesired behavior. Set the stage for the dog to commit the crime, so you know exactly what is going to happen. Then plan what you would do as if it were any other training exercise.

- What behaviors are you going to correct?
- When exactly are you going to do the correction? What is the timing?
- What methods should I use for the correction?

Does your dog steal food from the table when you turn your back? Put a sandwich on the table and stay away. How long do you think it will take before the dog nabs the sandwich? What kind of correction is best in this situation, a social correction or a surprise correction (read more about these later)? What do you plan to do afterwards? Will you move past it and take care of the dog? On the other hand, will you continue cleaning the house, totally ignoring the dog and what just happened? Surely, its not your fault that the sandwich attacked your dog?

Change the dog's thinking!

The right timing presumes your dog will understand why he is being corrected. Can you predict when the dog is about to do something wrong? Correct the dog's thinking! The chance of success in stopping the unwanted behavior is much greater if you intervene before the dog does something wrong than if the correction takes place after the behavior has already begun. Even if we successfully stop the behavior once, it may not result in any permanent change in the dog's behavior.

Quick corrections

In order to be effective, the correction must be quick. It should be as fast as pouring a glass of water. A correction that takes more than a second is in many cases entirely ineffective. The longer your correction takes, the greater the risk the dog does not make the right association. A lot can happen during a correction that takes too long. This means we may never really know what the dog actually associated with the correction.

If your dog runs up to another dog, and you don't correct him until he is on his way back to you, isn't there a chance he will then relate the correction to the idea that it is wrong to approach you? Or with the fact you get mad every time another dog pops up? The consequence may be that your dog no longer will come to you as willingly, but only after he takes the time to assess your mood. The wrong correction may also lead the dog to repeat the same action the next time around.

Breaks are necessary

Do not repeat your planned correction too many times in a row. Just when you are teaching obedience, we must provide breaks for the dog to absorb the experience. Make sure the dog is in a quiet environment during the break. It doesn't need to be very long – five minutes is enough. Then give the dog a chance to commit a crime to see if the correction had the intended effect. Does the dog refrain from the bad behavior? If he does, you just turned a corner. Now is the time to reward your dog for the behavior you wanted in the first place.

Corrections, when you lose your cool,
are seldom effective.

SOCIAL CORRECTIONS – WHEN YOU CAUSE DISCOMFORT

There are different types of corrections. Social corrections are those where the dog knows that you are the one doing the correcting. This can be anything from corrections with your voice or a look to threatening body language or physically grabbing the dog.

The most common correction is the "no". Correctly used, the word "no" is a good tool. A "no" means "do not even think about it" or "stop what you are doing right now". However, in the same way as happens with children, "no" will lose its value if we use it too much or if we do not follow through. A "no" should always be an unconditionally interrupting command. In other words, it sets a high standard.

So plan your corrections carefully! Look at "no" as an SOS-signal, something you only use with good reason. Personally, I do not consider teaching a verbal "no" very important, as a sudden clearing of the throat, a short sharp bark, or a growl will communicate to most dogs that it's time to terminate any bad behavior.

Always resolve a social correction

For the dog to understand a correction, we must be able to immediately read the signals when he "apologizes". So stop correcting as soon as the dog ceases his bad behavior and initiates contact with you. This lets you know whether your dog has understood your correction in the right way. It must pay off for the dog to discontinue a bad behavior!

After socially correcting the dog, always move away from him. This is how you give the dog the confidence and space to look for you. Moving away tells the dog that you are friends again. Think of the correction as a rubber band. You quickly stop the dog's bad behavior. Then turn and back up or move sideways, as soon as the dog turns and seeks contact. There is seldom any need to jump and skip. It is enough to stay friendly and calm. After all, you are your dog's security blanket, right?

One example of the "rubber band" is your behavior when your dog ignores your recall. Promptly run towards your dog in a fit of mock anger. As soon as your dog stops his incorrect behavior and turns towards you, slam on the brakes and back up as you call to him in a friendly way. Reward him with play, his favorite treats or maybe "just" with yourself. It must be worth it for the dog to obey a correction, and afterwards the dog shouldn't hesitate to seek contact with you.

The mortal sin – correcting for too long

Continuing to correct the dog after he no longer exhibits the improper behavior will eventually decrease his trust in you. He may choose to flee or increase the intensity of his behavior. He will chase and hunt even more, or lunge even more at approaching dogs. Stricter corrections are hardly the solution. He has no incentive to stop his bad behavior if he continues to be corrected.

Teach yourself to stop your correction at once and be friendly with the dog to discontinue the behavior. If the dog responds by avoiding us when we correct him, we have put too much focus on the correction and too little on removing the discomfort. A dog that will not spontaneously seek contact with you after a correction but instead repeats the mistake is neither stupid nor aggressive. It is just that he has not been given the option of forgiveness.

Repeated corrections – a sign of bad training

Sometimes corrections may have to be repeated on the same occasion. However, this is a corrective measure – not a preventive one. If the correction becomes a habit, then it's a symptom of something missing in the preventive training. We should not hold the dog responsible for this. If you find yourself in this type of situation, it is time to rethink your training plan.

Nova lunges at other dogs

I met Marie and Nova, a mixed breed of Maremma and German shepherd, when I taught a weekend course in southern Sweden. Nova had been re-homed, and nobody until Marie had given her direction and training. On the contrary, the woman who owned her previously had been afraid of Nova. Marie's problem was that Nova lunged at other dogs, even at a distance.

I decided that we should teach Nova passivity. We started by putting a treat in front of Nova when she was sitting. As soon as she stood up to take the treat, Marie grabbed her by the skin under the chin. She moved Nova's head upwards and backwards and at the same time pushed Nova's rear down. It was important that Marie performed the movements silently and calmly, like a visit to the veterinarian – neutral, friendly and crystal clear.

For the dog to feel comfortable with this training, we must release the skin of the chin as soon as the dog is quiet. Then we calmly massage and talk to the dog without staring at it. Continue to pet the dog on the neck with one hand, so you are ready in case the dog decides to charge forwards.

We repeated the training until Marie was sure of the technique. Then I distracted Nova by playing and joking at a distance. Nova took off, but Marie quickly grabbed her cheeks, turned her head backwards and pushed her butt down – fast, silent, with no aggression. It did not take long to see results. When she had mastered the technique,

Marie started doing the exercise at a distance from other dogs. The goal was to sit Nova down when she raised her ears and looked at a dog, before she lunged. Marie could take Nova for a walk that same evening and sit her down and massage her near other dogs. She still kept one hand near Nova's cheek, just in case she reverted to her old behavior.

Training tip:

Grabbing the dog's chin (as in the example with Nova) is a very useful correction if it is taught under calm conditions. You need external rewards to give to the dog once you say, "go ahead". For this method to work, you must learn the right technique and the timing. You must also practice planning ahead without irritation or aggression. Your attitude must be calm, deliberate, and confident. This exercise should be eighty percent about massage near whatever the dog is after – the why doesn't matter.

Reading suggestion: Read more about passivity training in the chapter "On/off! About environmental and passivity training"

SURPRISE CORRECTIONS – QUICK DISCOMFORT

A surprise correction is based on the idea that the dog doesn't have enough time to understand where the surprise comes from. What exactly it is that surprises the dog doesn't matter. It may be a cascade of water, or a newspaper or ball you throw. The main thing is that it's a surprise. Imagine you are sitting in peace and quiet, reading a book. Suddenly you feel a hand on your shoulder. You jump at the sudden touch. You turn around, only to find it is one of your children coming to you for a cuddle. The surprise was over in a flash, but you still had time to experience a short period of discomfort. A ball that suddenly hits the dog might have the same effect. It does not have to be followed by verbal corrections or sulky expressions. On the contrary, laugh and pretend as if nothing happened – what do you know?

Surprise corrections – easier timing

Often, surprise corrections have a stronger effect than social corrections. The timing and accuracy are easier. Social corrections often occur too late and go on for too long. In addition, surprise corrections have the advantage of the dog not associating the correction with you. A dog that keeps stealing food from the table will quickly learn to jump up on chairs and steal food, as soon as we are out of sight. After that kind of correction, you had better not show yourself. Otherwise, the dog will associate the correction with you as the bad guy. What will happen then if the food is on the table and you are somewhere else?

STATE OF EMERGENCY – WHEN NOTHING ELSE WORKS

There are times when I have disregarded all the above recommendations, for example, when there is an acute emergency, and another person or dog is the subject of a dog's aggression. Then it's no longer about teaching. However, we must use this type of correction with discretion. Acting first and thinking later may have huge consequences. In spite of everything, most situations are predictable. Therefore, we are usually able to plan corrections in the majority of situations.

SUMMARY

- A correction is just an action against something.
  Use basic obedience to prevent problems!
- Correct without value judgments – do not allow your emotions to guide you!
  Plan your corrections!
- Select a particular correction depending on your dog and the situation.
- Correct the thinking – once the dog has made the mistake, it is already too late.

When problems surface – turning conflict into control

Contents:

Conflict will inevitably arise in any human-dog relationship. Unresolved conflict, in turn, will create stress and anxiety. In most cases, the conflict will even reinforce the incorrect behavior, and cooperation ceases altogether. Most conflicts become ritualized in a specific situation or environment. In principle, it is possible to otherwise maintain a conflict-free relationship between owner and dog.

In many cases of conflict, the dog tries to avoid proximity to his owner. Flight behaviors are very common. Certain types of dogs react in a way that is almost stereotypical for their breed. A Belgian sheepdog, for example, is much more likely to flee than a Rottweiler. Instead, the Rottweiler often resorts to aggression. Other dogs turn inactive and freeze during a conflict. This is very common with golden retriever females, for instance.

There is a fine line between conflict and gaining control over a situation. In this chapter, I will discuss some common types of conflicts and how best to resolve them.

WHERE DO CONFLICTS COME FROM?

In some situations, we want our dog to behave in a certain way, regardless of whether we are in the vicinity or not. As I open the car door, I want the dog to remain behind. If I am consistent, the dog will learn not to jump out until he gets a "go ahead", regardless of whether I tell him "stay" or not. He learns, because the situation is always the same.

If we want to maintain control, we must be consistent. We must not leave room for misinterpretations. If the dog jumps out of the car as you open the back door, he must get back in just as fast. The dog doesn't get to decide what he prefers. It is not OK for the dog to sometimes jump out, and sometimes stay in the car. Which cues should we use to prompt the dog to jump out? Which cues tell the dog to remain in the car? Conflicts with dogs are often due to inconsistency in our cues for a desired behavior. Do not give him opportunity to misunderstand!

Staying on the property even when there is no fence

For awhile I lived in a house that had no fence around the property. In the summer, cars would drive by at high speed on their way to the harbor. It meant mortal danger for my dogs, if they were ever to put their paws outside the property boundaries. Therefore, I trained them never to leave the property ahead of me. I used the same principle as with the front door. The rules were clear: the dogs stay behind, I walk outside. When the coast is clear, I call them. I was always careful to leave the property using one of only two locations: a footbridge or a driveway. It was at these locations that I taught the dogs never to get ahead of me. My goal with this training was that the dogs would automatically stay behind me. The premise for this training to work was that I had to be 100 percent consistent.

Setting up clear rules gave me control over the situation. I was always leaving the property ahead of the dogs, and the dogs had to stay completely still before they were allowed to leave.

Reading suggestion: In the chapter "Become a better teacher – about learning theory" you can read more about how to teach commands that your dog will understand.

CONFLICTS OVER HUNTING BEHAVIORS

Many dog owners have a very naïve attitude about letting their dog "run free". Seldom do they realize the connection between running full speed through the forest and hunting. This means it will be a lot more difficult to stop the dog the day he decides to chase a wild animal. Sometimes people think it doesn't matter because the dog will never catch anything. Nothing could be more wrong! Dogs will indeed catch prey, especially when they are in good condition and the prey is weaker. This is the exact same premise as among wild animals. A dog who is not allowed to run free should be exercised on a long line, so he does not injure wild animals, other dogs or people. This is a matter of respect and consideration for everyone who enjoys the great outdoors.

Yelling will make the dog want to hunt more

Trying to teach the dog something when he is already focused on the hunt is often an exercise in futility. The dog is too closed off to learn anything. If the dog associates your "no" with your anger rather than his behavior, then you risk rewarding that behavior. Your "no" will have the opposite effect, and you will make the dog want to hunt more. Besides, your aggression will just worsen the relationship between you and your dog. In addition, there is a risk that your dog will then not dare to approach you when you are angry.

Reading suggestion: Read more about how to train your dog not to chase and hunt in the chapter "Tattling is terrific". In the chapter "Correction – or revenge?" you will find more about how to stop unwanted behaviors.

CONFLICTS OVER THE FRONT DOOR

When the doorbell rings, we often yell at our dogs and make a fuss. A dog with guard instincts could not draw any other conclusion than that it is the devil himself ringing the doorbell. A retriever, on the other hand, will react to this problem by becoming more and more excited. Somebody is here! Wow! In situations where you want your dog to be calm and composed, it is important to create rituals. It's better to start training when dogs are young to teach them what you want them to know for the rest of their lives. Thoroughly practiced rituals create control and help avoid conflicts.

Teach the dog to remain calm at the door

Here is one way to teach the dog to remain calm at the front door. Have him sit at a suitable distance from the door. He should not be in the way when visitors come in. Place a treat or a favorite toy on one spot and put on your jacket to go out. Little by little, vary the spot where you place the treat. If you have used external (previously placed) rewards in training before, then this exercise will be easy. In order to get his release command – "go ahead" - the dog must remain calm and still. There is no need for him to sit for any length of time. "Go ahead" means permission to eat the treat and accompany you outside, or to take the toy along on the walk. The dog learns to associate peace and quiet at the front door. This makes it easier to control the situation when there are visitors.

While some dogs are overjoyed at the prospect of visitors, others are not quite as enthusiastic. If you have a dog that is bred to guard, it is not fair to correct him for doing his job. Instead, praise the dog and give him a treat. Correcting the dog when you are in a foul mood often creates conflict. The dog becomes frustrated, which increases the likelihood he will be aggressive towards your guests.

Then train the dog to sit with a treat or toy in front of him while you ring the doorbell. Leave the door open so the dog understands that this is training. If the dog attempts to get up, correct him with a "no". When you can ring the doorbell and he does not move, reward him with a release command. Then have someone else ring the doorbell. At the same time, call your dog in a friendly voice and have him sit using a treat or a toy. Create a calm, quiet atmosphere and demonstrate that visitors are an occasion for fun.

There's the doorbell! Time for a bone!

Another way to teach your dog to stay calm at the front door is to teach him that the sound of the doorbell means a bone is on its way, in the same way as you teach him to respond to sound of the clicker. Most dogs will be more interested in a meal than in greeting visitors.

If your dog doesn't want to greet visitors at the door, let him instead have his bone in a different room. Then your guests can come inside in peace and quiet, and you avoid conflicts around the front door.

Reading suggestion: In the chapter "On/off! About environmental and passivity training" you will find more tips and ideas about how to calm your dog down. Information on clicker training can be found in the chapter "Become a better teacher – about learning theory".

CONFLICTS ABOUT CARE & GROOMING

Dogs are not exactly thrilled when you look down their throats, nor are they the biggest fans of having their nails clipped. The main reason for this is their dislike of being restrained. However, dogs need to learn to be comfortable when you groom or examine them. I have a lot of respect for veterinarians who have to examine reluctant dogs on a daily basis. If you establish examination as part of a daily routine, it will be much easier to teach your dog that having his heart listened to or throat examined is not a traumatic event. Moreover, the earlier you start this training, the easier it will be.

Teach your dog to accept medical care

Put your dog on a table and set out a treat he is not allowed to touch. As soon as the dog becomes passive, tell him, "go ahead." This will teach him to stay still to gain freedom and a treat. Repeat this exercise and examine his ears. Repeat, and look down his throat. When he becomes calm, tell him "go ahead."

In this way, you teach your dog that he can control the situation. Practice a few minutes each day, and you will not cause yourself, your veterinarian and your dog any unnecessary discomfort.

Loon, the diabetic monkey

The staff at the San Diego Zoo use clicker training. Loon, who was one of an endangered species, needed daily insulin injections to treat his diabetes. To make it easier to administer the medication, the staff started training Loon with the clicker. They clicked at the same time they fed him fruit. After a couple of repetitions, he approached the trainer to get his fruit when he heard the clicker.

Now the training really began. A long hollow tube was constructed in his cage. The eventual goal was to take blood samples through the tube to measure Loon's insulin levels. The first step of the training was to teach him that he got a click and a piece of fruit if he got closer to the tube. Once Loon had mastered this, he did not always receive a click for this behavior. He had to figure out how to get his caretaker to click again. It turned into a game between the caretaker and Loon. The monkey quickly learned to get closer to the tube. Gradually he became comfortable getting close to the tube, touching it, putting his arm into it, grabbing the handle of the tube and allowing another caretaker to scratch his arm. They were finally able take the blood sample. He also learned to accept insulin injections in his behind. So training your dog to put up with having his nails cut should be easy, right?

Gaining comfort with strangers

Many dogs don't like to let strangers handle them or look in their mouth. It is possible to train your dog to get over this by having the dog watch while you hand a treat or a toy to the person who will examine his teeth. As soon as this individual has the treat, he or she should walk away and hide the reward. Then he or she should return and stand far enough away so dog doesn't feel threatened. At the same time, as soon as the dog makes eye contact with the stranger, he or she should give the dog a release command – "go ahead" – to find the treat. Repeat the exercise until the dog anticipates the command and thinks the interaction is a fun game. Then the stranger should gradually move closer to the dog before saying "go ahead." Take it one step at a time until the dog is totally comfortable with the situation. You should try this with different people and in a variety of environments.

Then have your assistant to place his or her hands on the dog. If the dog remains seated, your partner will reward him with a release command. Gradually vary the duration before the release command is given. Otherwise, there is a risk that the dog will perceive the hand as a cue to search for treats. Once again, repeat the exercise with different people and in different situations.

The next step is for your helper to walk up, pet the dog and bare his or lips on one side. If the dog remains still, reward him by allowing him to search for the treat. Be prepared to backtrack occasionally in the training, particularly when you introduce an unfamiliar person or environment. After awhile, the dog will become more comfortable with the ritualized situation and have an easier time allowing strangers to examine his mouth, as the entire situation now represents something positive. In this way, we turn conflict into control.

Reading suggestion: In the chapter "Help! My dog growls!" and "On/off! About environmental training and passivity training" you can read more about conflicts surrounding grooming and care of your dog.

CONFLICTS OVER MEETING OTHER DOGS

There are plenty of impolite dogs, and just as many impolite dog owners. Some firmly believe that their dog has a god-given right to bound up to other dogs. Of course, I have a right to decide when and if I want my dog to spend time with other dogs. This is particularly important in situations where other dog owners we come across allow their dogs to decide – often with the justification that dogs know better than people.

I disagree with the notion that dogs organize themselves into a dominance hierarchy. It is indeed important that my dogs should be able to lie down beside other canines without feeling threatened. Nor should not being allowed to play with other dogs be a source of stress for my pet. I have no interest in allowing adult dogs to spend an evening together when I am invited out for dinner. That sort of encounter would probably not result in the establishment of a permanent pack. The risk of conflict is too great if you only plan to allow your dog to interact with another on a single occasion.

Choose the right playmate for your dog

In the same way as we want make the world safe for our children, so we should choose dogs – especially puppies – that foster a sense of security. Your dog shouldn't have to deal with a bully. Bullying or biting is always an act of aggression, where the owner is always the one responsible.

However, inexperienced dog owners may have difficulties recognizing what is appropriate in certain situations. Generally speaking, most dogs are fairly apprehensive when their owners are out of sight. It's an even trickier situation if a dog jumps a fence from his own yard and attacks another dog. If you live in an area where aggressive dogs are not always on leashes, there is not much you can do except trying to avoid the situation. How do we know when its okay unleash our dog and allow him to greet a strange dog? We don't. This situation becomes about how quickly you can "read" the other dog. If you are an inexperienced owner, this can be very difficult.

Most encounters between adult dogs turn out just fine, particularly when the owners are walking in different directions and don't get excited. If there is an encounter, do not immediately look for injuries, unless there is an emergency. Take down personal data and phone numbers from the other dog owner. Whatever you do, don't yell and scream, as that often is more traumatic for your dog than the attack itself. Convey that its time to get up and go on. If possible, have your dog interact with another dog of the same breed that attacked your dog as soon as possible. Sometimes we can be biased against certain breeds, which we then pass on to our own dogs.

Your attitude affects the encounter

The older literature on dogs maintains dog owners should never avoid an encounter as that would demonstrate fear. The problem has to do with how our dog understands what we are communicating when we choose to walk directly up to the approaching dog. How will the dog interpret your behavior if you are afraid or insecure, and still walk straight up towards the source of your fear? Will your dog understand what makes you afraid or angry? If you are angry, will your dog understand that you are angry with him and not with the other dog, or vice versa? Your own attitude affects the outcome of any encounter. We dog owners often make things a lot more complicated than is necessary.

Your attitude affects not just your dog, but also the person or animal you encounter. It is hardly accidental that certain dog owners are barked at during walks. What message are you sending – calmness, lack of control, aggression, joy? Focus on your own emotional mood in encounters with other people and animals. Create the right conditions for a calm encounter! If "heel" doesn't work – avoid the command, change your emotional mood and speak "dog" instead. What emotion do you want to convey to your dog and others you may encounter?

Lunging at other dogs

A couple with a female Rottweiler contacted me because their dog had started lunging at other dogs. I asked how they usually handled encounters with other dogs. The husband told me he shortened the leash and commanded the dog to heel. This worked up to the point of the actual encounter. Then the Rottweiler would throw herself to the end of the leash against the other dog, barking madly. This dog also happened to be very fond of food, so after stuffing my pockets with chicken we started on our walk. Every time she caught sight of another dog, I immediately pushed my fist with some pieces of chicken against her nose. I took away my hand and quickly threw five, six pieces within an area of a few square feet that she then was asked to search. She forgot all about the other dog, and the most important thing was to find food.

Resolving emergency situations

Can it be this easy? Shouldn't we teach the dog that lunging is not allowed? The truth is that we often make things much more complicated than they actually are, rather than looking for the easiest solutions. When you make a habit of using your usual voice commands to stop the dog's actions rather than initiate positive activities, they lose their usefulness. The same holds true if they don't work in an emergency. Therefore, it will be a lot better to resolve the situation by teaching the dog something completely different.

In the case of the female Rottweiler, she learned to look at her owner so that he would allow her to look for scraps of food. In this way, he gained control over his dog and mitigated the conflict. We can apply the same kind of training to bicyclists, joggers and other distractions we encounter during our walks.

The best thing with this method is that you teach the dog to initiate the behavior himself – making contact to get treats – without any prompt from you. Dogs who are disinterested in other dogs will often pretend to be interested in sniffing the ground. The other dog notices this and remains calm. Therefore, these kinds of encounters seldom result in conflicts, compared to a staring contest between two angry dogs.

"Nibbling encounters"

Personally, I teach my puppies that encounters with people, dogs and other animals always mean food, which I give from either side. I prepare for an oncoming encounter by taking something yummy out of my pocket. Preferably, this should be something extra special, especially when the encounter is particularly difficult. Use your dog's favorite food to speed up the learning curve.

As the other dog or person approaches, I push the treat against the dog's nose without saying anything. During the encounter itself, my dog walks beside me, nibbling on tiny little pieces of treats from my hand. A small dog can jump. I focus on a calm and positive emotion and smoothly walk forward. Consistently positive encounters will teach the dog to seek contact with you when he catches sight of something. He will learn to "tell" to get his reward. So don't forget the treats when you want to teach your dog about positive encounters.

Reading suggestion: In the chapter "Play – and tell me who you are" you can read about play and cooperation between dogs. How you teach your dog to tell is described in the chapter "Tattling is terrific".

"Stop!"

Contents:

"Stop" may be the single most important command you ever teach your dog – even more important than "here". "Stop" is a command to stop the dog in his tracks, no matter where he's headed. The dog must be able to stop anywhere, both when he is moving towards you and away from you. For many dogs, it is easier to stop than to come on a recall command, because it is often difficult for him to let go of whatever it is he is looking at.

"STOP" – AN INVITATION FOR FUN

Most dog owners use the command "stop" primarily to get the dog to stop, not to initiate an activity or play. However, if we always say, "stop" only to interrupt the dog's actions, then eventually he will stop only to find out what is going on around him. "Something popped up! What am I looking for?" Instead teach the dog to "stop" as an invitation for fun!

Continue to give rewards – or the command loses meaning

Do you often yell to make the dog stop on command? Are you often angry when you finally catch your dog? If you are, you might lose his trust when you tell him "stop". You will teach him to associate "stop" with your anger.

You must make sure there is a balance between what you offer the dog for stopping on command and what you require of him in a questionable situation. If you stop rewarding your dog with play, treats or some activity, you risk undermining the value of the command. Put away your feelings when the dog defies you. Instead, figure out exactly how your dog understands "stop". What can you do to change your dog's response to your command? Should you be firmer with him – or teach him to equate "stop" with fun if he pays attention immediately?

REINFORCE NATURAL BEHAVIOR

There are different ways of teaching "stop". One way is to reward the dog when he stops spontaneously. Begin your training during walks. If the dog slows down on his own and waits for you, reward this behavior by immediately throwing a treat or a toy over and beyond the dog's head. I usually keep a reward in my hand to be able to reinforce the behavior as soon as the dog spontaneously offers it.

Catching the behavior is an interesting method of teaching "stop", as it is based on motivation and joy. In addition, encourages the dog to initiate cooperation and offer obedience. More and more frequently, the dog will then display the behavior to see if he will get a treat or two.

Flying rewards

It is important that you throw the reward over the dog's head at the same time as you tell him "go ahead". This prevents the dog from seeing you as the source of everything fun. As a result, he won't move towards you but stay where he is. As soon as you notice that he is stopping on his own to see if you will throw a reward, add a verbal "stop". Reward him immediately with a "go ahead" as soon as he freezes, and throw the treat.

Training tips: Look for the right expression

When you teach your dog to "stop", you should also observe his expression when you reward – not just the fact that he is standing still. Should he actively look at you, or do you want him to just stand there looking calm? What is the position of his ears? Is his tail still or is he wagging it? I want my dogs to stand still and look at me attentively.

PLAY "STOP"

You can also make "stop" into a game. My golden retriever Mio learned to stop when I crouched like an animal lying in wait. When Mio saw me crouching as if I were going to leap, he became completely still. As soon as I made a swift move in any direction, he came rushing towards me. He growled playfully, and we rolled around in a wild wrestling match.

Command "stop" when the dog does something right

Give a verbal command of "stop" the moment the dog halts. Reward him immediately with "go ahead" and a new game. In the beginning, your verbal command will have no meaning to the dog, as your body language is the basis for his learning. Continue training and your dog will learn quickly.

Never say "stop" until the moment your dog stops moving and stands still.

Otherwise, your dog will mistakenly associate "stop" with activity. Test it now and then by commanding "stop" while the dog is moving. Does he stop? If so, then he understands the command.

Reading suggestion: Read more about how you can use "go ahead" as a reward in the chapter "Become a better teacher – about learning theory".

It pays off to stay still

You – not your dog – should be the one to release him from "stop" and reinitiate activity. No play starts again until you say, "go ahead". Remain passive and look away if your dog becomes impatient and tries to start a new game. Otherwise, you will reward the dog for being active, rather than staying still. Moreover, your dog might also make the wrong association with your command. Instead, teach him it pays off to stand completely still. Then he will begin to understand "stop".

Gradually expand the exercise. Give the "stop" command and quietly take one step away from your dog. If he stays, release him by telling him "go ahead" and start playing again. Remember that what is new and difficult for the dog is the moment you start moving. If he manages to stay still, immediately tell him "go ahead" and start playing with him again. Do not halt before you give him a reward. It is not your body language but your verbal "go ahead" that should release him from the position. Now you will also find out how accurate you have been in giving the command at the right moment. If you were careless and commanded "stop" when you stopped yourself, the dog might believe that "stop" is all about your behavior.

Make your dog anticipate "go ahead"

You may recall that in the beginning it was your playful body language that made your dog stop. Now when you try to teach your dog to remain standing despite your movement, it is easy for the dog to misunderstand your actions as the start of a new game. Therefore, it is essential to make very subtle changes in your body language. The method for teaching this command is based on a hunting game. It is important that you maintain a balance. Do not excite the dog by using sweeping gestures but maintain some excitement in the situation. Move like a cat sneaking up on a prey, softly and cautiously, but still on target. Spellbind the dog, keep him focused, waiting for your "go ahead". Don't let him know exactly when you plan to start playing. Walk, run or crawl. Teach your dog to focus on your words rather than your body language. This will keep your dog's attention on verbal commands rather than your actions. Anything can happen – whenever. However, "stop" is always "stop".

Stop before you have too much fun

Do not repeat this exercise more than a few times during the same training session. The dog's attention and motivation may decline with too many repetitions. This method is based on fostering interest and curiosity in your dog. Stop the game while your dog still wants to continue, and he will be more 'on' and excited for the next training session. He will also learn more quickly.

TEASE OUT THE BEHAVIOR

You can also tease out the behavior and make the dog stop by pretending to throw a ball to him. The dog will probably dash away after the ball, only to find it is not there. Most dogs will then stop and look around wondering, "Where is it?" Reward him by throwing it him and saying "go ahead". Occasionally repeat the exercise during the walk, but be careful to actually throw the ball most of the time. Otherwise, you teach your dog not to leave until he is sure you have actually thrown the ball.

Add a verbal command

At the exact moment when your dog goes from moving to being completely still, tell him "stop", lift your arm, simultaneously telling him "go ahead" and throwing the ball over and beyond his head. Make sure he is actually still when you say "stop", otherwise he might associate "stop" with movement. Continue the training so that your dog stands still for a second or two before you throw the ball. Then switch up when you give him the reward. You can even test your training by taking a few steps towards your dog before you say "go ahead" and throw the ball.

Remember to introduce one step at a time. Start by increasing the amount of time before he receives the reward. If the dog makes a move towards you, do not correct. Instead, take a time-out – stop playing for a moment.

Did your dog understand?

Now you are ready to see whether or not your dog has understood the meaning of your verbal command. Pretend to throw the ball again. When the dog dashes off at full speed, say "Stop!" If your training has been successful, your dog will slam on the brakes and seek contact with you. If he stops, but immediately starts moving again, then he has not yet fully understood the meaning of "stop". Then it's time to continue the training. Vary the amount of time before the dog gets his reward, before you try adding the command when the dog is in motion.

Distractions increase understanding

When the dog understands the verbal command, it is time to take the training even further. During a walk, tell him to "stop" when he is walking or trotting ahead of you. If he slams on the brakes, reward him as before and give the release command "go ahead" as you throw the treat or the ball.

Build on the training by adding small distractions. The more disruptive the distractions are, the more important the rewards become. Do not correct the dog if he cannot handle the distractions. At this stage, your dog is able to "stop" in a quiet environment, but he still has a lot to learn.

Refresher courses

Teach him to "stop" in wide variety of situations. Make sure you don't reward him if he doesn't immediately stop or if he starts walking towards you after a few seconds. Always be prepared to repeat the first steps of the training program now and then to refresh his memory, even if the dog is older and well educated. Do you remember everything you learned in high school? Dogs also need refresher courses.

TEACHING "STOP" WITH TRAINING LURES

When we teach him to "stop" with training lures, we don't make the dog figure out how to get his reward but we help him. This method presupposes your dog knows the meaning of "go ahead".

Sit down and place a hand on the dog's chest. At the same time, place a treat in front of him. Say "stop" in a calm and clear voice. This should not pose any problems if you have taught "go ahead" earlier on, and if your dog understands he needs to be calm before getting a release command. If he doesn't understand, repeat the training for "go ahead" before you start teaching "stop". Remember it is always your dog's passivity and calm attention that will lead to "go ahead". Reward him as soon as he is still.

Repeat this exercise a few times during the same training session. If the dog still tries to nab the treat, quickly pick it up and deny him his reward. Gradually take away your hand and use only "stop". If the dog doesn't display the desired behavior, just pick up the treat. Alternatively, put out your hand to stop the dog.

Reading suggestion: Read more about learning theory with training lures and how you can gradually phase out the lures in the chapter "Become a better teacher – about learning theory".

Training in natural environments

Whenever possible, use natural environment when you teach him to "stop". This will help generalize the dog's knowledge. Good training opportunities are by the front door, the car and the edge of your property. Rocks and stumps in the woods also make good training lures. Let the dog jump up on a large rock, tell him "stop" and throw out your reward. Your dog will eagerly wait for your "go ahead", so he can be allowed to search for his treats or favorite toy. Gradually, the dog will try to jump up on rocks and stumps by himself. He will lure you with a "stop" and subsequently a chance to play.

During a walk, you can turn "stop" into a game by using the command in a quieter and quieter voice. In order not to miss out on an exciting activity, your dog must keep close to you. For example, trick your dog by turning and walking in the opposite direction. When the dog runs past, whisper "stop". If your dog is not paying attention, do not repeat the command. The opportunity for teamwork and fun and games will have vanished for this time.

Do not be afraid to let the dog guide you to an activity. This will build teamwork!

USE DISTRACTIONS TO TEACH "STOP"

When your dog knows how to stand still, start adding distractions to create even greater comprehension. "Stop" can be associated with many different situations! Get up slowly and see if he is able to remain still. The challenge will be the moment you start standing up, not when you are fully erect. If the dog stands still, reward him with "go ahead" at the same time as you move. Remove the treats if you see the dog even contemplating moving.

Most dogs get excited and move around when we pet them. This is one kind of distraction. Try moving around in front of the dog. If he is able to stand still for few seconds, reward him with the "go ahead" and let him take the treat on the ground. Use your imagination to find different distractions, so you can teach your dog as many different "stop" scenarios as possible. Get family members and friends involved in the training. Somebody can come up and pet your dog or play with a ball as he stands still. In my classes for young delinquents, the students dance with each other and even play with another pooch in the vicinity of the dog who is to remain still. However, do not make the exercise too hard. Increase the distractions gradually. Learn to read the dog and help him succeed.

Do not waste your time figuring out how "good" he is. His knowledge and understanding will be apparent in how well he manages the increasingly distracting situations.

Think about:

In what situations and environments do you want your dog to "stop"? When you open the front door? At the edge of your yard? When you open the car door?

Train your dog at a distance

Train your dog with distractions even when you are a few feet away from him. Start close. Then you can always correct him as the slightest twitch of movement. Continue to give the release command for the right behavior, no matter where you are in relation to the dog. Use different distractions at a variety of distances! Sit down and eat a sandwich, or have someone in the family jump up and down in front of the dog while you run away. In the beginning, reward the dog immediately for the correct behavior – standing still, calm and attentive.

Make sure that the reward is really valuable to the dog, who will be more motivated to stand still regardless of distractions. Bring a treat or toy and train him in different environments, where natural distractions occur. The more distractions you have taught with your dog with at home, the easier it will be for your dog to recognize what he is supposed to do.

Ritualized rewards result in worried dogs

Be sure that you never stand with the same posture or on the same spot in relation to your dog when you give the release command. Otherwise, dog might think that "go ahead" can only be given when you stand in a certain position.

This will decrease his understanding of the release command. If you ritualize your position when you say "go ahead", your dog might be inclined to respond with activity, as he thinks the reward is on its way.

Many dog owners go back to the dog before they reward him. This is why some dogs never become secure in staying still. This is partly because it takes too long before the he gets his reward; partly he always gets his reward when we are beside him. The dog becomes very eager when we get close and starts getting anxious and has a hard time staying still. This is because the dog gets his reward in the exact same way all the time, instead of in association with the correct behavior.

Training tips:

Work with a variety of training methods at the same time. This will help the dog understand more and he will learn what "stop" means more quickly. In addition, it is more fun for both of you.

SUMMARY:

- "Stop" is perhaps the most important command you can teach your dog.
- Teach your dog that "stop" means fun.
- Reinforce the right behavior – it teaches you to read your dog's body language.
- Play "stop" – you can make training into a game.
- Work with distractions. Generalize the dog's knowledge!

"Here!"

Contents:

A good recall is the sum of your relationship with your dog. The recall grows out of the obedience and play. Accordingly, it is not a single event. The social cooperation between you and your dog must function for the dog to always respond when you call him. A dog that associates you with fun eagerly anticipates play and games when you call him – and comes bounding joyfully.

THE RECALL – SOMETHING FORBIDDEN OR COOPERATION?

Our own view of recalls doesn't always agree with that of the dog. For you, does the recall mean the dog should stop what he's doing and come to you? Do you call your dog when he is having fun? If you don't offer any interesting alternatives to what your dog is currently doing, your dog might perceive your recall command as something negative – you force him to interrupt his fun.

If your dog doesn't come when called, you will seldom solve the problem by becoming exasperated and correcting him. He will then respond by moving towards you in an attempt to appease you. The dog may also run away to avoid the correction. If the dog moves toward you when you correct him, it's not necessarily wrong – but the dog might learn not to come unless you are mad. That's hardly what you want him to associate with the recall, right? Irritation will never increase how quickly he comes!

Recalls – invitation for fun

The prerequisite for a good recall is thus teaching your dog that spontaneously making contact with you is positive. If your dog has not learned that it pays to be willing to follow, it will be considerably more difficult to teach him to come when called. It is essential you reward the dog's spontaneous desire to seek contact, otherwise the dog might stop a bit away from you, avoiding closeness, no matter what you entice him with. Recalls are based on cooperation! So continue to reward the dog for spontaneously seeking contact with you for the rest of his life.

Reading suggestion: Read more about how you train your dog to be obedient in the chapter "Who follows whom? About contact and obedience training."

Train recalls under the right conditions

It is easy to think of other things during a walk. Suddenly your dog is gone! This is when our interest perks up – where did he go? Quite often we start training recalls under the wrong conditions, like when the dog is off leash and busy doing his own thing. In this situation, the odds of a successful recall are few. The dog will either have the wrong association – or none at all – with the recall command.

Reading suggestion: Teaching the dog to tell is a great supplement to recall training. Read more about this in the chapter "Tattling is terrific!"

ATTENTION, ANTICIPATION AND COMMANDS – THE FOUNDATION OF RECALLS

Before you start teaching your dog recalls, it is helpful to break the training down into several parts:

- The dog should turn his head and seek contact with you when you call him. He should pay attention to his name or some other cue, previously decided on.
- The dog should early anticipate being close to you and should expect some kind of reward.
- He should learn a recall command that means he should run to you.

If these basic criteria are satisfied, a successful recall is extremely likely, even when the dog is far away.

Think about:

Which step should you focus your training on?

Reading suggestion: In the chapter "Close to me – about greetings", you will learn more about how to strengthen the dog's desire to be near you. Read about how to build a stronger relationship with your dog through play in the chapter "Play – and tell me who you are".

TEACH THE DOG TO PAY ATTENTION

Dogs quickly learn whose voice is the most interesting to pay attention to, and they filter out all the rest. For the dog to respond in all situations, we must teach him to make a positive association with the command. We don't like it when our name is used in an irritated or aggressive tone of voice – why would your dog think any differently?
The goal of the recall is to be able to control your dog in any situation. Therefore,

the dog has to get something he wants out of the training. Otherwise, we might think the dog is being stubborn.

Attention is not the same as the recall

An attention command does not mean that the dog should come to you, only that he should turn his head and look at you. Get started indoors by teaching the dog whatever attention cue you plan to use. This could be the dog's name, a whistle signal, or any other sound you choose. Just be careful never to use that particular cue in any other situation than attention training.

Teach your dog to pay attention indoors

Start by having the dog in front of you. Give the attention cue and give the dog something he responds positively to, such as a treat or a ball. As long as the dog is an active participant, he is learning something. Do the exercise in short spurts, one to three repetitions, and then take a break. Like in all kinds of training, depending on the individual and the breed, it is important that you carefully read and understand the dog's signals for him to assimilate what you are teaching. Don't keep going if the dog is not interested in the learning process.

When the dog understands that the attention cue means the appearance of some type of reward, you can increase the difficulty of the exercise. Say his name or give the cue when your dog is busy doing something else. He should be nearby, but his nose should be pointing away from you. For now, you should still be in a distraction-free environment. As soon as the dog turns around on your cue, throw the treat or ball to him. You could also spit out the treat, or sit down so the dog can take it from your mouth.

Remember that the dog should get his reward on the spot where he is, for example by throwing it to him. You are not teaching recalls quite yet – you just want the dog to learn to pay attention and listen for his name!

Outdoor training

Continue to work in the same way, only move the training outdoors. Hold your sessions in a variety of situations and in different environments. Your dog should turn his head and look at you before he receives his reward. Don't repeat the cue if he does not immediately respond. The prospect of a reward is simply gone. The correction consists of not being allowed to play with you and not getting any reward at all.

Next, train your dog off leash or with a long line dragging behind him. Give the cue at various distances at the same time as he moves around in front of you. Once again, the dog gets his reward only when he looks at you immediately.

Then shake things up. Vary the type of reward you give him – sometimes verbal praise is enough. Your dog shouldn't be able to predict his reward when he hears the cue!

Ignoring distractions

Now it is time to teach your dog to pay attention even when there are distractions. Try giving the dog the attention cue at the moment he catches sight of a car, or some other passing distraction. Don't pull or jerk on the leash, as the dog might learn that your cue, together with distractions, means something unpleasant. Your dog might then lose the positive association he has already made with his name. Practice when you meet other people and dogs, as well as in a variety of environments.

You can also make the training more difficult by whispering your dog's name. This teaches him to listen for quiet cues. The goal is that your dog should become keenly sensitive and motivated to listen for your cues in any environment.

If the dog doesn't pay attention the first time, don't repeat the word or give him a reward. If the dog then makes contact with you three seconds later, pretend you never said anything. Instead, figure out why it didn't work and what you can do differently next time. Having control over the teaching situation is an important requirement for learning, so the dog learns to associate your cue with the correct behavior.

Stop and smell the roses

Build on your training so the dog learns to listen even when he is busy sniffing something interesting. If you cannot make your dog pay attention to your cue when he is on leash, neither is he likely to obey you when he's off leash and you have nothing to pull on. Be consistent when you reward him. The dog should immediately seek contact when you give the cue.

Say the dog's name when he is sniffing something interesting. Throw a few treats to him as soon as he makes contact with you. This kind of training will produce a dog who eagerly anticipates something delicious from you. Soon you'll have a dog who responds even while he is sniffing. Owners of male dogs often find themselves in conflict with their dogs that become preoccupied with odors. This results in nagging and annoyance, which isn't pleasant for anyone.

Correctly trained, your dog will learn he does not always have to abandon those exciting scents, but that you may offer something even better. In this way, there will not be any competition or conflict about the sniffing. This kind of training is both simple and incredibly effective. Throwing a treat to make the dog search is in many cases a lot better than giving him a treat from your hand, as the search itself stimulates the dog. Make sure the dog actually looks at you before you throw the treat. Otherwise your dog will learn to search for treats when you say his name.

Vary the rewards

As soon as your dog quickly makes eye contact when he hears your attention command, begin to vary how you reward him. Sometimes he is allowed to search for treats that you have thrown on the side of the road. The next time, reward with petting and cuddles. A third time, maybe tell your dog to "sit", so you can tell him "go ahead" and throw him a toy or a treat. Try changing the situations and never reward him if he doesn't immediately make contact.

Training multiple dogs

It is one thing to teach your dog his name when he is an only child. When you have several dogs, things get trickier. One simple way is to say the dog's name instead of "good", when one of the dogs is to get a treat as a reward. If anyone else in the pack begs for a treat, hold your ground. Correct dog + correct name = treat.

Begin the training when the dogs are sitting or standing in front of you. They will quickly learn to wait their turn. Then try saying their names when they are turned away from you or doing something else. Say the name and throw or give the treat to the dog in question as soon as he turns his head towards you. If the dog doesn't make contact, don't repeat his name but continue with one of the others. The dog you spoke to first simply misses out on the treats.

You can even place a treat in front of each dog when they are sitting and then say his name and "go ahead" to the dog who is to get a treat. By using fun exercises such as these, you will create order and harmony in your pack, as well as dogs who know their names.

A word of warning about competition over food. Pay attention to how far apart the dogs are and allow them to sit or stand on the same spot. Also, train each dog individually so that everyone understands the exercise before you train them all together in a group.

TEACH THE RECALL COMMAND

Train the recall command in tandem with the attention cue. This recall command, like "come" or "here" or a whistle, means that the dog should not only look at you, but also come running to you.

When you teach your dog this command, start by turning and walking away from him. Give the command right as your dog starts running towards you. You can reinforce the command by simultaneously showing the dog you have something fun that he wants, preferably something you have on a string and can pull on the ground. Then the dog will learn to associate "come" or "here" with fun.

Give the command only when the dog is in motion

Be careful not to use the recall command when the dog is standing still. Moreover, don't tell the dog "come", only to later run away if he doesn't come. If you repeat this few times, you might teach your dog what Kipling in the example below was incorrectly learning: "come" did not mean for him to come. It meant that his owner would run away!

Kipling's passion

When my golden retriever Kipling was a young adult, I lived close to a lake that we often walked around. That is where we practiced obedience training and fetch in the form of search exercises and hand signal exercises, both on land and in the lake. Kipling loved water and often ran spontaneously into the lake to get me to initiate some kind of water game. Sometimes I would do what he wanted and sometimes I just kept walking. It was difficult to get the water-crazy dog out of the lake, and like many others, I made the mistake of telling him "come" in a situation where I had no control. The consequence was that I had to walk away while Kipling stayed in the water. After a while he understood that I was not about to play with him, so he came running after me. This behavior was repeated and I quickly realized that I was teaching him a very different cue for coming when called than what I intended. "Come" made Kipling ready for me to leave him. The recall command that actually made him come was me turning and walking away.

Once I realized this, I changed my approach. I left without saying anything. I shouted "come" at the exact moment he started to gallop after me. After a number of repetitions, Kipling made the correct association with "come". He obeyed my verbal cue without me having to walk away.

THE FINISHED RECALL

You have finished your recall training when you make the connection between the attention cue and the recall command. When the dog looks at you, give him the attention cue together with the recall command: "Kipling, come". If the dog comes, reward him by throwing a ball or something else he wants behind you. This will simultaneously teach the dog to run quickly on his way in. When the dog begins to understand, you can vary when you throw the ball: sometimes at once, sometimes halfway through and sometimes not until the dog has come all the way up to you.

Remember that recalls are not about preventing the dog from what he is doing but instead are a promise for fun. Practice recalls by hiding behind a tree and having your dog hunt for you. Show yourself when you notice that he is getting worried and give him the recall command.

A dog that associates you with fun eagerly anticipates play and games when you call him – and comes bounding joyfully.

See the parts in the whole

A complete recall consists of many different parts that all must be maintained. If you always reward him only when he reaches you, then you are really only reinforcing the last part of the recall. Thus, the dog has to display a chain of different behaviors before he gets his reward: raise and turn his head, turn his body, start moving towards you, run all the way and then finish up by approaching you. Vary how and when you reward him to reinforce the dog's familiarity with all the parts of the recall!

Use variation

Many owners find their dogs come quickly when recalled, but then they dart away just as fast. Perhaps he has learned that the best way to get our attention and earn rewards is to run away. That's when we call him! One dog owner laughed when I described this during a lecture. Her dog ran away and stood behind trees and bushes, anticipating her recall command. The woman had made a habit of calling her dog when she disappeared out of sight. As a result, the dog associated her invisible owner with getting a reward.

Can a dog really reason this way? This is not about thinking. Instead, it is about the fact that we have called the dog many times in similar situations. Although the dog has learned to come when called, we have also inadvertently taught him that he should run away to get the recall. You have consequently established an unintentional behavior chain: running away results in recalls – which result in rewards.

Training tips: the 80-percent rule

If you want to increase the contact between you and your dog, then call your dog eight times out of ten when he looks at you or approaches you – not when he is leaving you.

DISTRACTION TRAINING AND WORD COMPREHENSION

You should also teach your dog that the reward can come from other places than your hand. You might place the treat somewhere between you and the dog, or perhaps behind you, ahead of time. Your dog is not allowed to take the treat until he has sought contact with you – and not until you have given the release command "go ahead". Vary the time between giving "go ahead", verbal praise and the recall command – sometimes as the dog sits there waiting to be called, sometimes as he is on his way towards you and sometimes as he reaches you. This is good recall training for several reasons. On one hand, you are training your dog to listen for the command separately from distractions in a controlled environment. On the other hand, you are teaching your dog to differentiate between "good" and "go ahead".

Work with one distraction at a time

Expand your distraction training by working with one distraction at a time. For example, have a person stand somewhere in between you and your dog and have him or her distract the dog. In case the dog interrupts the recall itself, this person should remain entirely neutral. Then, repeat the recall. Even here, you can vary the straight recall with "go ahead". This teaches your dog to listen and be attentive to possible changes during the recall. Perhaps you will have a friend playing with her dog somewhere during the recall, for example when your dog is waiting for you, or why not behind you? If your dog runs up to his friend without permission, shoo him away and start over. Your dog should pay attention to you and obey the recall to receive "go ahead" and permission to play. Use your imagination – what distracts your dog? Can you use the distraction as a reward? Allow him to run away to his reward when he demonstrates the correct behavior? Can you reward your dog when he comes up to you without him misinterpreting it as a "go ahead" and taking off?

Reading suggestions: More about how to use "go ahead" as a reward can be found in the chapter "Become a better teacher – about learning theory".

"NICE HAND" AND "PING PONG"

It is actually possible to teach the dog to come without giving a verbal command. Stand still and place some treats or toys close by. Wait until your dog spontaneously comes up to you and discovers the treasures. Repeat this exercise a couple of times. It will give you a silent command for the recall – namely that you are standing there straight. Alternate this by standing still with a toy in your hand. As your dog approaches, invite him to play. As soon as he understands he is to come back when you stand still, switch it up and vary when and how you reward him.

The recall command "nice hand"

Dogs are not always fond of human hands, which can grab his face and take hold. More than half of the dogs in my classes back up or halt as we reach out to them. One dog will duck to evade our hand when we call him; another will back away when we reach to take the toy from his mouth.

Instead, make your hand a tool in the recall training instead of an instrument for grabbing. The principle is simple. Sniffing your empty palm leads to a treat from the other hand. When the dog understands this, start throwing the treat in different directions so that the dog runs away searching for it. For your dog to get another treat, he must return and put his nose on your palm – again and again.

Start this exercise indoors by sitting on the floor or a chair. Keep a couple of treats in your one hand, and then hide both hands behind your back. When the dog is quiet and focuses on you, reach out with one of your hands to within four inches of the dog's cheek. As soon as the dog turns his head and sniffs your open palm, praise him and give him the treat with your other hand. Both hands then disappear behind your back right after the reward. Wait until your dog is calm and focused and has stopped peeking for more treats before you reach out towards the opposite side of the dog's cheek. Vary which hand you use for the treat and for the cue. Repeat three to five times before taking a break.

After few successful trials, it is normal for the dog suddenly to remain sitting, seemingly not understanding anything. Quietly count to five, and then hide your hand behind your back. After a couple of seconds, test him by reaching out again. Do not practice this for more than two or three minutes. Then change places by standing up or slowly moving forwards or backwards. When your dog understands that, he is to push his nose against your palm, trying to put your hand on other areas near his head. Vary the treats with offers to play.

Your hand – a positive place to run to

As you increase the distance between you and your dog, you can throw the treat in different directions instead of giving them to him. To get the treats again, the dog must run back to you and push his nose against your hand. Use this game to teach a cue for recalls.

As the dog approaches spontaneously, give him the cue – your open hand. Start by showing the cue when your dog is nearby, and then show your hand earlier and earlier. When your dog understands the meaning of this cue, he will approach faster and faster to push his nose against your palm. Continue varying where you place your hand: high, low, while moving, to the right, to the left, etc.

Of course, this kind of training will not replace verbal recalls. But it teaches our dogs to look at us much more frequently so as not to miss the recall cue. In other words, the dog will be more prone to seek contact with us so as not to miss out on anything. Never mind how impressive it looks when your dog comes tearing like lightning when you show your palm! The advantage with teaching the dog to push his nose into your hand is that you no longer need treats, which can be a distraction. Your dog will be much more focused on the task at hand. The greatest benefit is that your dog will not back up when a hand reaches out, but instead he will actively look for it regardless of distance.

"Nice hand" can be used in many different situations:

- As a silent recall cue, associated with your dog seeking contact.
- During encounters and meeting people, as the dog may walk with his nose in your hand.
- When playing fetch where the dog is supposed to drop things into your hand. If the dog already knows to put his nose into your hand, the training will be easier.
- As a tool for teaching the dog to follow your hand, to sit, lie down or stand when you are using hand signals to direct the dog from a distance, or teaching the dog to crawl in more advanced obedience training.

"Ping pong" teaches speed and encourages anticipation

A couple of years ago I learned a simple and fun exercise for contacts and recalls from a Swedish colleague, Kickan Allendes. I call it "ping pong". This exercise is a lot of fun for both owner and dog. It also creates faster speeds. This exercise for recalls and contact is based entirely on action. No stopping anywhere along the way. Have fun!

Start by placing yourself on a smooth surface indoors or outdoors on asphalt or gravel. This is important mainly in the beginning, later on the ground surface will matter a lot less.

1. Throw a plainly visible treat so it lands within ten yards of your right.
2. Right as the dog picks up the treat from the ground, call him, and at the same time throw another treat so that it lands within ten yards of your left. Make sure the dog can see the treat so he doesn't stop to search for it.
3. Repeat the exercise, switching between your right and left side and varying the distance you throw the treat.
4. Generalize this training by repeating it in different environments and situations.

SUMMARY

- A well-taught attention cue often also leads to good recalls.
- The recall command should stir up anticipation for fun!
- Annoyance and frustration will not increase the speed of the dog's recall.
- Only reward your dog when he comes immediately and quickly. You shouldn't reward him for "long and faithful service".
- Vary your rewards, for instance when he looks at you, during the recall itself and as soon as he comes to you.

"Sit!"

Contents:

All dogs "know" how to sit. But, do you know what cue makes your dog sit? Does he understand when you tell him "sit"? If you turn your back and tell him "sit" - does he still understand? We don't know what association the dog really makes when we teach him something. If you teach "sit" while holding a food bowl, there is no way of knowing which cue makes him sit. His behavior is often tied to the situation or the environment, not to our verbal command. Does your dog know "sit" without his food bowl and in a different environment?

Routine teaching situations, using the same body language and in the same environment, will teach the dog one thing. If the situation changes, the dog may no longer understand what we mean. Generalizing the dog's knowledge determines how he will understand the meaning of "sit" in other situations and environments.

CHOOSE A CUE FOR "SIT"

When you put your hand in your pocket to get a treat is perhaps the most common cue for "sit". A hand signal may work; it doesn't nag to the extent that our voices often do. However, it may also mean that many dogs don't understand "sit" if they are looking in a different direction.

Decide from the start which cue or cues you are going to use for "sit". It is equally important to decide which cues are not going to trigger the behavior. For example, if you don't want your dog to sit when you put your hand in your pocket, then don't give him a treat for that – otherwise you reward the dog for paying attention to the wrong cue.

SHAPING OF "SIT"

There are many different ways to teach "sit". Shaping is my favorite way of teaching a multi-step process, as the dog becomes the central actor in his own learning. If you want to participate in obedience competitions, it becomes extremely important to teach the dog to be persistent in working for his reward.

Teach the dog how the method works

First of all the dog needs to learn how shaping works before you start teaching him to associate particular words with particular actions. Sit down and show the dog you have a treat in your hand. Wait for the dog's spontaneous attempts to get the treat. Hold your hand on your thigh so he can't bump your hand out of position. That turns the exercise into a hunting game, which won't work. If the dog tries to manipulate you into opening your hand by chewing on it, don't give in. Keep your hand still!

When your dog spontaneously takes a step back, maybe looking at you or releasing your hand for a second, open your fist and immediately give him the treat. Reward even the slightest indication of cooperation. The dog should not stand 30-40 seconds without something happening as he will become frustrated. He might become impatient, start barking or whining or lies down. In this case, the situation is too much for the dog to handle.

Reward the thought – not the final behavior

Repeat the exercise a few times and open your hand with the reward only when the dog does something right. Now the dog has learned he only gets the treat when he doesn't bite or bump your hand. The next step is to make the dog understand there are several things he needs to do to get his treat. You should remain passive and silent. This method is based on the dog actively seeking various solutions. What odes he have to do to get his treat?

Imagine a house made of building blocks. That is your finished "sit". During the shaping process, you must envision all the little pieces that will build the finished house. The fewer segments you use to build the house, the greater the risk of collapse. If the dog makes any attempt to lower his rear, you must be quick to reward him. Don't wait until the dog actually sits. It is the thought of sitting that you should reward!

When your dog understands he gets his reward for lowering his rear a bit, then delay gratification and let him test things out a little more. Reward him as soon as he actively lowers his behind even more. Step by step, you will shape your dog to sit down.

Add the command when the dog has understood

When the dog offers the behavior on his own, it is time to add the command "sit".

Tell him "sit" right as he sits down.

Varying the number of treats will also teach him to stay for more. Every time you put the treat in his mouth, repeat "sit". This increases the likelihood he will associate his behavior, i.e. sitting, with the cue word and the reward. Then lure him to get up before he gets up on his own.

Shaping – challenging but effective

Does this seem difficult? Shaping puts great demands on you and your ability to read your dog, but it also gives deeper insights into the dog's mind. You can quickly know whether you actually rewarded the behaviors you intended to teach the dog. If training were limited to two minutes at a time, it would force us into thinking through exactly what we want to teach the dog and how to do it. Shaping techniques make us understand that a behavior most often consists of a series of steps. When we realize this, our teaching process becomes more effective. In addition, the dog's understanding will increase – and thus the reliability of the cue.

Reading suggestion: Read more about shaping and the learning process in the chapter "Become a better teacher – about learning theory".

TEACH "SIT" USING TRAINING LURES

Another way of teaching "sit" is to use training lures. Start the training by taking a treat in your hand and silently move it over the dog's head. Can you make him sit as you intended? Tell him "sit" and give him the treat the moment his hind quarters touch the ground. This helps the dog to make the right association between action and word. Pull back your hand immediately after giving the dog the treat. If the dog continues to sit without stretching for your hand, immediately give him another treat from your other hand. Tell him "sit" again as you give him the treat. This makes the cue word synonymous with the reward.

Then lure the dog into getting up and repeat the exercise a few more times. If the dog sits just as you intended, give him a treat from your other hand and at the same time say "sit". Only use treats as a reward, not petting or verbal praise, which will just distract the dog at this stage of the learning process.

If you want to use only a verbal command, try saying "sit" without raising your hand. If you have been careful in saying "sit" at the exact moment as the dog's rear touches the ground, and you varied which hand you use to give the treat, the dog won't usually have any problems understanding what you mean.

Alternatively, you can do the opposite – keep the hand as a cue and don't bother with a verbal "sit".

All dogs "know" how to sit.

Getting rid of the training lures

The dog will be fixated on your hand in the beginning and not conscious of his own actions. This fixation will disappear by varying which hand you use to reward him. In addition, you decrease the likelihood he will follow your movement and get up as you withdraw you hand. If the dog makes a mistake, don't correct him but instead try to become aware of what it was you did wrong.

TEACH THE DOG TO SIT QUICKLY

We usually want the dog to react immediately and quickly when we say "sit". Don't get annoyed if the dog sits down slowly, as he will then slow down even more to calm you down. The most common reason why dogs sit slowly is that they don't quite understand what to do. This is often in combination with dominance and nagging from the owner: "sit, sit, SIT, SIT!" Concentrate on getting the dog to move fast – your verbal command is not important at this stage. You may possibly have to change to another word later, a command with which your dog doesn't have the wrong association.

Play makes for faster movements

Dogs also sit down slowly because we have rewarded the slow sits. If you want your dog to sit faster, try bumping him playfully so he gets up on his feet. Joke around in a happy and taunting tone of voice, and at the same time stick a treat under his nose and swiftly move a few steps away. Most dogs will become more active if we playfully taunt them. Say "sit" again and see if the dog sits down faster this time.

If the dog fails twice in a row, you have to figure out why he doesn't understand. Are there too many distractions that keep him from focusing? Examine yourself – does the dog understand what you mean? For your dog to learn to sit quickly, he will need a reward *every* time he sits fast during the training

If the exercise fails repeatedly, analyze how the dog perceives the cue for "sit". What exactly did you teach him?

Fast sits using a ball

Another way to increase the speed of the sit is to pretend to throw a ball so the dog runs a way a bit. When he turns around to ask you where the ball is, tell him "sit". As soon as he sits, throw the ball and at the same time tell him "go ahead". Don't do this exercise more than once at a time and sometimes throw the ball instead of saying "sit". Otherwise, the dog learns that the ball won't come. He will then eagerly stand in front of you rather than sit. If the dog moves towards you when you say "sit", don't throw the ball. Taunt him a little instead and continue on the walk.

As the dog starts to understand what you mean, become selective and only reward the best performances. Is it fast enough? Let the dog know what he has missed. This will encourage him to try harder next time.

"SIT" WITH DISTRACTIONS

When the dog understands "sit", it is time to start introducing distractions into your training. Have the dog sit and hold a treat in your hand a little away from him. If he gets up, quietly take the treat away and start again. As soon as the dog no longer attempts to grab the treat, tell him "go ahead" and allow him to take it.

Then test him by placing the treat on the floor, and allowing him to have it if he remains seated. Make the training more difficult by throwing the treat behind your dog, to his side, or in front of his nose. Does he understand which command lets him get up and take the treat? Can he handle sitting still even when you excitedly praise him? Does he remain still if you cuddle and pet him? Good, now you really are starting to teach your dog the meaning of "sit" regardless of environment or situation.

Training tip:

It is sufficient that your dog ignores a distraction twice before moving onto a new distraction.

Train distractions before distance

Make sure your dog can handle sitting in spite of nearby distractions before you leave him sitting at further distances. The distance often becomes a minor problem for a distraction-trained dog. What happens if the dog makes a mistake and gets up? Quickly grab the treat from the ground. Withdrawing the reward is usually enough to tell the dog he has done something wrong. Training should be fun for both of you, right?

Reading suggestion: Read more about how you can use the release command "go ahead" as a reward in the chapter "Become a better teacher – about learning theory".

SITTING AT A DISTANCE

It can be useful to be able to tell the dog to sit, even when he is a bit away from you. Start by making the dog stand beside a bowl of treats and take a few steps away. Tell him "sit". If he does, tell him "go ahead". If the dog goes for the treats, remove the bowl and start over.

Then gradually increase the distance between the two of you, but be prepared to alternate between "go ahead" and "sit", as soon as the dog starts understanding the exercise. Otherwise, your dog will sit down as soon as you bring out the bowl. The cue for sitting then becomes the bowl, not your verbal command.

Instead, try placing the food bowl in various positions in relation to the dog. Place it four yards to the left or to the right of the standing dog – or even behind him.

Train by throwing a treat

There is another way to teach him to "sit" at a distance. Silently throw a treat for the dog to look for. Say "sit" when the dog has eaten it and looks at you. Reward the correct behavior by saying "go ahead" and throw another treat or a toy over the dog's head. Be sure to vary when and with what you reward. If you always reward him in the same way, at the same point in time and on the same spot, it will become a ritual. If and when you break the ritual, your dog might stand up.

Instead, teach him that you may release him with a "go ahead" at any time. Interrupt the "sit" only when your dog calmly follows you with his eyes, not when he restlessly moves his paws or turns around.

Teach your dog to watch out for cars

Throwing a treat before saying "sit" is a good method for teaching the dog to watch out for cars. Throw a treat away from the road when you see a car coming. Say "sit" once the dog has gobbled it up. Throw out a new treat that you don't allow him to get up and eat. Then reward him by allowing him to search for the treats, once the car has passed. If you practice this consistently, your dog will gradually learn to associate cars with jumping to the side and sitting.

Remember to vary exactly when you say "go ahead". If you always give the dog the release command as soon as the car has passed by, after a number of times the dog will see the car as a cue to stand up, not your "go ahead". Make sure that your "go ahead" keeps its meaning.

Above all, this method is useful if you go for walks where there aren't many cars. In city traffic, the most important thing for the dog to learn is to stop at the edge of the sidewalk, before being allowed to cross the street.

Training tip:

The dog will learn faster if he hears the cue word repeated during the learning phase – particularly in association with getting a treat. In addition, "sit" will acquire a double meaning, as it also means treats. This is a more positive association than if you just say "good" when you give him the treat.

SUMMARY

- Decide from the start which cues you want to use to tell the dog to sit and which ones he is to ignore.
- The dog should associate "sit" with his own action and not with a particular environment. Teach him to "sit" in many different situations!
- Don't get annoyed if the dog sits down slowly.
  That will slow him down even more!
- Vary how you reward him and what you use.
- Teach him to ignore distractions! Increase the distance only when the dog knows how to sit in spite of distractions.

“Down!”

Contents:

What cue will make your dog lie down? A verbal “down”? When you point to the floor? Or when you put your hand in your pocket and bring out a treat before giving the cue?

A major source of conflict between owners and dogs is not being careful enough in teaching the dog exactly which cue is to trigger what behavior. Your dog doesn't understand the cue for “down” until he knows to lie down regardless of your body language. Teach your dog to understand the cue word, regardless of whether you are sitting, lying down, standing, walking or holding something in your hands.

SHAPING OF “DOWN”

There are several methods for teaching “down”. The shaping of “down” involves the dog figuring out how to obtain the reward. This type of learning process mentally challenges the dog. He must figure out on his own how to get you to give him the reward – while you remain passive.

Sit down on the floor and let the dog know that you have a treat hidden in your hand. Keep your hands still against your stomach. Wait quietly for your dog to try to get at the treat. Keep your hand still and ignore it if the dog nibbles or paws it. Reward him instead when he takes a short break. Teach him it doesn't pay off to try to steal the treat!

Shaping "down"

When the dog realizes that nagging is not going to get him the treat, he might sit down and "think about it". This starts the shaping process, where you gradually form the dog's behavior. Reward him if he chooses to sit. Then wait for your dog's head to start dropping towards the floor. Reward him at once with the treat. Continue to reward every intention in the right direction – towards the floor. If the dog stands up when he doesn't get a treat, ignore it and continue rewarding unprompted sits until he stops moving in the wrong direction.

Work in silence and do not use any words to interrupt the dog. Instead, make it a guessing game – what behavior will get me a treat? Gradually demand a little more by withholding the reward if he doesn't try a little harder. Then he will gradually come to understand that the point of the game is to get closer to the floor. After a few repetitions, he will know he doesn't get a treat until he lies down.

Reading suggestion: You can find more about shaping and other teaching methods in the chapter "Become a better teacher – about learning theory".

Teach a verbal command

When your dog understands that the point of the game is to lie down, it is time to pinpoint the behavior. Do not say "down" until the dog lies down completely. Only then can he really associate "down" with the act of lying down rather than standing or sitting. Give a treat at the same time as you say "down".

If your dog gets up, ignore him. Wait until he lies down again, repeat "down" and give him a reward. By learning this way, the dog learns to associate "down" with keeping his body against the ground. "Down" also means getting a treat.

Teaching at this stage should be as uncontaminated as possible and free from unnecessary talk and other distractions; all that will just confuse the dog. Rather repeat "down" and the treat a couple of times as your dog is lying down.

Lying down on command, not on his own initiative

Now it is time to teach the dog to lie down only when you give the command. Sit down and say "go ahead" while you throw the dog a treat. When he returns and stops in front of you, tell him calmly and clearly "down", once. Wait in silence for your dog to lie down. As he touches the floor with his whole body, immediately repeat "down" and give him a treat. Release him with a "go ahead" and throw a treat for him to run after. Repeat the exercise a few times before taking a break.

Then vary the length of time before you say "down". The dog should learn to wait for the command before he lies down. It is quite likely that he will resort to lying down before you give any command. Then do a 180-degree turn away from him and take a brief time out. When he pauses for a split second before lying down, say "down". Your "down" will then function as a reward for waiting.

Wait a second longer each time so the dog learns to wait before you say "down". This makes the dog eager to hear "down" as it is accompanied with a reward. Thus, "down" goes from being a spontaneous, unprompted behavior to something you control. Be sensitive and responsive and don't let your dog lie down spontaneously more than once. Give him a chance to succeed! Don't overestimate your dog's ability to wait or he may become frustrated. It is like skipping first grade and going straight to second; it produces anxiety rather than understanding.

Build your dog's knowledge

After teaching your dog to respond to "down", start giving the command in different situations, both indoors and outdoors. Just because your dog understands "down" in the kitchen doesn't guarantee he will understand it elsewhere.

Build your dog's knowledge by gradually changing your own position. Sit on a chair and tell him "down". Give the command when your dog looks away in another direction or perhaps while a family member is petting him. Teach your dog that "down" and a reward may appear in any situation. Your playful training will build your dog's knowledge and desire to cooperate – even under more distracting circumstances.

TEACH "DOWN" WITH TRAINING LURES

Another way of teaching "down" is to use training aids and clearly show the dog what to do. Hold a treat in front of your dog's nose when he is sitting. Then move your arm straight down and out along the floor in an L-shaped movement. Stay silent!

Say "down" and give him the treat as soon as he lies down. Release him by throwing another treat with a "go ahead". When your dog comes back again, repeat the exercise.

Using training lures means there are several cues for the dog to associate his behavior. He may perceive your hand signal as the cue, rather than the word "down". This creates confusion: is the cue the hand signal, the verbal command or the treat? Dogs often lie down on cues other than those we have in mind!

Reading suggestion: You can find how to gradually decrease the use of training aids and finally do away with them altogether in the chapter "Become a better teacher – about learning theory".

THE FIRST COMMAND IS THE ONLY ONE!

Teach the dog that the first command is the one he should pay attention to. If your dog doesn't lie down on your first command, start taunting him a bit. Show the dog a treat, but don't let him have it. I use this simple but effective method a lot in my teaching. Playfully taunting the dog a little is incredibly effective when it comes to making the dog understand the importance of the first command.

This method can be used also to make the dog lie down faster. Praise the dog for lying down, even if his reaction was slow. At the same time as you praise him, flash the treat in front of him but don't let him have it. Turn around – and start all over again.

"DOWN & STAY" WITH DISTRACTIONS

When "down" works fine, start prolonging how long you wait to give the dog the treat. This will teach the dog to stay lying down a little longer before he gets his reward. So now, you are teaching a new behavior: "down & stay". By giving one treat at a time when he gets it right, he will gradually stay down for longer periods of time.

Use the reward as a distraction

When you teach the dog to stay down in spite of adding a distraction, he will understand the exercise even more. At the same time, he will stay lying down for longer. The simplest way is to use the treat as a distraction. Place a treat several inches in front of the dog's paws. Tell him "go ahead" when he lies there calmly and attentively. Don't make him look at you before you give the release command. The important part is that the dog lies down quietly. When your dog understands how he is to behave, you can wait for his spontaneous eye contact before saying "go ahead".

Allow the dog to succeed, but also let him fail. If the dog gets up before you say "go ahead", make sure you quickly remove the treat and start all over again. If your dog tries to steal the reward, quickly put your hand or foot on it. There is nothing to be gained by stealing!

Reading suggestion: You can read more about distraction training in the chapter "Become a better teacher – about learning theory", which is about the learning process. There I also describe the difference between praise and the release command "go ahead".

Variation is the mother of knowledge

Test the dog by letting the treat fall from your hand – does your dog remain lying down? If he gets up, quickly snatch the treat, taunt him a little and start all over. Use distractions such as getting up, moving the treat around and talking. Can you stand up when the treat is on the ground? Can you run around and jump without the dog taking it? Can you pet your dog while he is staying down? Is he able to distinguish between praise and "go ahead"? Gradually introduce more and more distractions to build his understanding. Variation is the mother of knowledge!

Training tip:

Think in images! If you just teach the dog one image, i.e. a single situation, then he will have a very limited knowledge about what to do. Think about teaching as an old-fashioned roll of film and try to teach "down" in at least a dozen different situations. This makes it more likely your dog will associate "down" with his own actions rather than with a specific environment.

Basic won't stay still

Rickard had problems with his flat-coated retriever Basic, who was reluctant to stay down as his owner approached. Rickard had previously become angry and attempted to correct Basic when the dog wouldn't remain still. Now he just wanted to flee whenever Rickard approached.

We decided to try a different approach. Rickard placed Basic's ball a couple of yards behind the dog. Then he left. When Rickard approached the point where Basic usually took off, he gave Basic permission to run to the ball with a "go ahead". Rickard had to learn to say "go ahead" before Basic started displaying signs of anxiety, such as putting his ears back, yawning and licking his mouth. Basic slowly became more confident and Rickard could gradually get closer to his dog before saying "go ahead".

The solution did not focus on "down & stay", but rather in creating a common activity around the ball. Thus, Basic learned to stay lying down without the "down & stay" command becoming the focal point. The problem was solved when Rickard switched focus from correction to cooperation.

Repeat the basics as needed

It is not enough teaching the dog to lie down at home on the kitchen floor. You also need to teach your dog that "down" always means "down", regardless of what you are doing or where you are. Be prepared to repeat the very first basic exercises in a new environment or situation. Wait to add the cue until the dog displays the behavior on his own.

Training tip:

Do not make teaching "down" too difficult! Make sure he succeeds much more often than he fails during training.

SUMMARY

- Work silently until the dog understands what to do.
- Teach the dog that the first command is the one he should pay attention to.
- Train your dog to understand "down" regardless of where you are or what you are doing.
- Teach the dog to lie down despite distractions.
- Repeat basics exercises in new environments or situations.

CRAMO

Notes

*"We don't stop playing because we grow old;
we grow old because we stop playing."*

GEORGE BERNARD SHAW